LET YOURSELF GROW

How Neuroplasticity, Repetition, and Intention Shape Who You Become

DANIEL JARVIS

Copyright Page

Let Yourself Grow

ISBN: 979-8-234-18236-4

Independently published.

Printed in the United States of America.

For more works by the author, visit:

www.danieljarvisbooks.com

Formatted with Vellum

Contents

To my children,
May you always have the courage to learn, the patience to grow, and the wisdom to become the person you are meant to be.
With love,
Dad

A Note Before You Begin

This book repeats the same core truths through different stories, metaphors, and angles. That's not accidental — that's the point.

You're about to experience the principle this book teaches. While you read about neuroplasticity and how repetition builds neural pathways, the book itself is rewiring your brain using that same method.

Each chapter approaches the same truth from a different direction — a parable, a movie character, a personal story, a scientific principle. These aren't repeats. They're reinforcements.

By the end, you won't just know that repetition matters. Your brain will have learned it.

Introduction

The reason I wrote this book is simple: I'm fascinated by neuroplasticity.

If you've read my other books, you already know I weave it into everything — not because I'm trying to, but because it's the one thing I'm absolutely sure has shaped my life.

When I first heard Andrew Huberman say, "It's never too late to learn a new trick — neuroplasticity can happen no matter how old you are," something sparked in me. I didn't know much about the brain at the time. Honestly, I still don't know everything. But what I have learned is this:

Patterns are everywhere.

In movies.

In books.

In nature.

In the way people talk, move, grow, and fall apart.

We're all connected — not in a mystical way, but in a practical, observable, neurological way.

And once I started seeing those patterns, life got simpler.

I stopped getting upset so easily.

I became calmer.

I started noticing how everything fits together if you're willing to look at it differently.

We all connect with different ideas. What makes something click for one person might completely miss for someone else. That's why this book uses different stories, metaphors, and angles — because the brain learns through variety.

Sometimes a scientific explanation opens a door.

Sometimes a simple image or a silly metaphor does the heavy lifting. Growth isn't one-size-fits-all, so I wrote this book to offer your mind multiple perspectives on the same truth.

That's why I'm writing this book.

Because the way I see the world — the way I approach goals, habits, identity, and change — didn't come from talent. It came from years of reading, learning, failing, trying again, and watching how the brain rewires itself through repetition.

Intention started as something silly. But sometimes the silly things are actually signals — your brain's way of saying, "Pay attention. This is the thing you're supposed to write about."

What flows easily for me might not flow easily for you. But you have hidden talents that flow in other areas — and every one of those talents started with a spark, a choice, a repetition.

And repetition?

That's neuroplasticity in motion.

At the end of this book, you'll find something I call **The Growth Toolkit** — a collection of worksheets, reflections, and practical exercises designed to help you take these ideas off the page and into your life. Think of it as a place to practice the patterns, strengthen the pathways, and build the identity you're growing into. Books can inspire you, but practice rewires you. The Growth Toolkit is where that rewiring begins.

Life is nothing but an inter-web of emergence, and what emerges from life is infinite. Growth comes from chaos, and chaos comes with wisdom.

Daniel Austin Jarvis

1

The First Thought of the Future Self – Intention

If you've made it this far, you're probably wondering why this book is called Let Yourself Grow. It's called that because so often, we're the ones holding ourselves back. We settle into the complacent zone — comfortable, predictable, safe. This book shows you how to step out of that zone. It shows you how to let yourself grow.

Before we talk about growth, we have to talk about the moments that shape it — the quiet ones, the unexpected ones, the ones that don't look like growth at all. Sometimes the lesson shows up in the smallest places, like a morning that doesn't go the way you planned.

The Clock That Didn't Wake Me

The clock ticked, and the clock tocked, steady as ever.

But today, it didn't make a sound.

No alarm.

No jolt awake.

No command to rise.

It simply let me sleep.

Maybe it wasn't the clock at all.

Maybe it was something deeper — the universe, my body, my subconscious — all agreeing that today I needed thirty extra minutes.

A pause.

A breath.

A softer start.

Sometimes life protects you in ways you don't notice.

Sometimes the day begins late on purpose.

And when it does, you learn something important:
On days when you're thrown off schedule, you don't rush — you prioritize.

You do the most important thing first.

You cut the noise.

You focus on substance.

You fit in what you can and let the rest fall away.

This parable isn't about a clock.

It's about learning to move with the day you're given — not the day you planned.

It's about trusting that sometimes a late start is the exact start you needed.

Every time you decide to do something new, you're planting your future, not in the ground and not with your hands, but in your mind. A mental planting is the first seed of who you might become. It starts with thinking, imagining, procrastinating, questioning, and analyzing. All of that is the early spark of the new you forming beneath the surface.

What you choose to do with that spark determines everything. If you ignore it, it dries up. If you overthink it, it never breaks through the soil. But if you take that tiny spark and turn it into action, you begin shaping a real path forward. The seed becomes a direction. The direction becomes a decision. The decision becomes movement.

But thoughts without action don't create identity. They don't build habits. They don't form new neural pathways. They sit there, like seeds left in a packet — full of potential but never planted. Eventually, they turn into another one of your minions — another half-started version of you waiting for you to either nurture it or abandon it.

A seed only becomes a new version of you when you act on it. Action is what turns a spark into a pathway, a pathway into a habit, and a habit into identity. The future you starts as a seed, but it only becomes real when you decide to grow.

A late start teaches you to move with the day you're given. But every day also gives you a chance to plant something new — a spark, a direction, a beginning. One of my beginnings happened in a gym, with a barbell, long before I knew what it would grow into.

The First Deadlift

The first time I ever tried a deadlift, I wasn't trying to be strong.

I wasn't chasing numbers or testing anything.

I was learning something new.

My coach showed me the basics, and I lifted what felt natural. I didn't push it. I didn't try to prove anything. I just wanted to move well and not get hurt.

At the time, it didn't feel like a big moment.

But looking back, it was a perfect example of neuroplasticity in motion.

My brain had never coordinated that pattern before — the hinge, the grip, the breath, the timing. That first rep was nothing more than a weak electrical signal traveling down a brand-new pathway. A dirt trail in the woods. Uncertain. Unfamiliar. But alive.

That's how every new identity begins.

Not with mastery.

Not with confidence.

Not with a perfect rep.

With a spark.

A single moment where your brain says, "This is new. Pay attention."

That quiet first attempt didn't make me a lifter.
But it planted a seed — a humble one — that would eventually grow into something much bigger, simply because I kept showing up and letting the pathway strengthen over time.

That's neuroplasticity.

That's repetition.

That's how the new you begins — not with a dramatic moment, but with a small one you almost overlook.

That first rep wasn't strength — it was wiring. It was the moment a brand-new pathway lit up, weak but alive. And that's exactly how every version of you begins, not with mastery, but with the science happening underneath the surface.

The Science of Becoming:

Every version of yourself begins with a thought.

Before there is a runner, there is the thought of running.

Before there is a writer, there is the thought of writing.

Before there is a healthier version of you, there is the thought that change is possible.

Thoughts are the seeds of transformation.

But a seed sitting on a shelf never becomes a tree.

A thought sitting in the mind never becomes a life.

Something has to happen next.

Action.

The moment a thought becomes action, the brain begins a process of physical change. An electrical signal travels across networks of neurons.

Neurotransmitters are released. Communication begins. What was once only an idea now has a pathway through which it can travel.

This is the first spark of becoming.

Neuroscientists often describe neurons with a simple phrase:

"Neurons that fire together, wire together."

The principle, originally associated with psychologist Donald Hebb, holds that when groups of neurons repeatedly activate together, the connections between them strengthen. The more often a pathway is used, the easier it becomes for the brain to use that pathway again.

In other words, thoughts may plant the seed, but action waters it.

Intention is often what creates that first movement.

When we decide to act, the brain recruits systems involved in attention, motivation, and goal-directed behavior.

Neurotransmitters such as acetylcholine help focus attention on the task at hand.

Norepinephrine increases alertness and prepares the brain to respond to meaningful challenges. Together, these systems help transform a passive thought into purposeful action.

But one action alone rarely changes a life.

The real transformation comes through repetition.

Repetition is the nutrition of growth.

Every time you repeat a behavior with intention, the brain receives another signal about what matters. Another layer is added. Another connection is strengthened.

At first, the pathway is weak.

Like a trail through an untouched forest, it is difficult to follow.

The first run feels difficult.

The first workout feels awkward.

The first page feels impossible to write.

The first healthy meal feels unfamiliar.

But each repetition clears the trail a little more.

Over time, the brain responds by increasing efficiency.

Neural pathways become more coordinated.

Communication becomes faster. The cells responsible for producing myelin begin wrapping frequently used pathways with additional insulation.

Myelin functions much like the insulation around an electrical wire. It allows signals to travel more quickly and more efficiently.

Neuroscientist Daniel Coyle describes myelin as one of the biological foundations of skill development. The more a pathway is used, the stronger and more efficient it can become.

This is one reason habits often feel automatic after enough repetition.

What once required tremendous effort begins to require less conscious thought.

The behavior becomes part of who we are.

And that is where many people misunderstand change.

They believe transformation begins when the habit becomes easy.

In reality, transformation began long before that.

It began with a thought.

A thought became an intention.

An intention became an action.

An action became a repetition.

A repetition became a pathway.

A pathway became a habit.

And a habit slowly became an identity.

The opposite is also true.

Thoughts that never become actions eventually fade.

Ideas that are never practiced weaken.

Pathways that are never used become less accessible.

The brain is constantly adapting to what we repeatedly do and repeatedly ignore.

Neuroscientist Joseph LeDoux summarizes this concept well by explaining that the self is not fixed. We become who we are through experience, learning, and repeated patterns of behavior.

That means identity is not something we discover.

Identity is something we build.

Every choice is a vote for the person we are becoming.

Every repetition lays another strand of insulation around the pathway.

Every intentional action strengthens the architecture of the future self.

Once you understand how identity forms in the brain, you start seeing it everywhere — in every skill you learn, every habit you build, every new version of yourself you try to grow into. One of the clearest examples is something as simple as learning to forage.

Real-World Example: Learning to Forage

Imagine you decide you want to learn how to forage for edible mushrooms and wild plants. You hike through the woods and see mushrooms growing everywhere. Some may be safe to eat. Some may be poisonous. Looking at them, you can't tell the difference.

Instead of guessing, you buy a field guide and start learning. You compare the mushrooms you find to the pictures in the book. You learn about gills, spores, colors, habitats, and lookalikes. You also talk with experienced foragers who can teach you what to look for.

At first, every mushroom looks the same. Over time, you begin noticing patterns. The more you study and practice, the easier identification becomes. What once felt confusing slowly becomes familiar. You didn't become a forager the day you walked into the woods. You became a forager the day you decided to learn.

The truth is, learning to forage isn't really about mushrooms. It's about how growth works. You don't become skilled by wishing — you become skilled by learning, practicing, and showing up. And the same pattern applies to every part of your life.

Application to Your Life

Potential is a lot like an unopened book sitting on a shelf.

The information is there.

The lessons are there.

The opportunity for growth is there.

But if the book is never opened, none of that knowledge can help you.

Many people do the same thing with their own lives. They have goals to pursue, skills to learn, and dreams to achieve, but they never take the first step toward learning what they need to know.

Whether it's improving your health, starting a business, learning a trade, strengthening a relationship, or developing a new skill, growth begins when you're willing to open the book.

The future version of yourself is waiting inside the pages of the lessons you haven't learned yet.

The question is simple:

What book do you need to open next?

Reflection Questions:

1. When life throws off your schedule, who do you become?

Think back to a time when your alarm didn't go off, your plan fell apart, or your day started late.

Did you abandon the thing you intended to do, or did you adapt and make space for it anyway?

What does that reaction reveal about the identity you're building?

2. When you want to grow, do you plant one seed or scatter a whole packet?

Think about a time you tried to change multiple habits at once.

Did you thrive, or did you burn out?
Now think about a time you focused on one habit with intention.

Which approach helped you grow more deeply — and why?

3. When you miss a day, do you lose momentum or rebuild it?

Everyone has off days.

When you've slipped before — whether for a day, a week, or longer — did you return to your goal or walk away from it?

What will you choose next time the cycle dips?

4. What is the next version of you trying to emerge?

Name the goal, habit, or identity shift that keeps tapping you on the shoulder.

What is the seed you're ready to plant?

5. What is the first action — the spark — that will bring this seed to life?

List the smallest, simplest step you can take to begin.

Not the whole plan.

Not the perfect routine.

Just the first spark that tells your brain, "This matters. Strengthen this."

Growth always begins inside you — with a spark, a seed, a pathway forming long before anyone else can see it. But eventually, every inner change asks for something more: a life to grow into. And that's where Chapter 2 begins — with the moment you stop preparing to become the next version of yourself and finally step into it.

2

The Meatball Parable-Becoming

How often do you let yourself grow?

How often do you sit there and let your growth stagnate?

Here's the secret:

Growth starts with repetition.

Repetition becomes discipline.

You can see this pattern everywhere in nature — but nowhere more clearly than in the life of a bee.

The Bee of Consistency

Out in nature, nothing shows up more consistently than the bee.

It doesn't wait for motivation.

It doesn't negotiate with the day.

It wakes up, gathers pollen, collects nectar, and returns to the hive.

Then it does it again.

And again.

And again.

One trip doesn't make honey.

One day doesn't fill a comb.

One moment of effort doesn't build anything meaningful.

But repetition does.

When the bee shows up day after day, the hive fills.

The nectar becomes honey.

The work becomes something sweet, something real, something earned.

And the bee doesn't just make honey — it spreads pollen everywhere it goes.

It helps other things grow without even trying.

That's what consistency does in your life.

When you show up for your habits the way a bee shows up for its hive, you build something over time — something you can taste, something you can feel, something that lasts.

And just like pollen, your good habits spill into others.

People see your growth.

They feel your energy.

They take a little of that "pollen" and start growing themselves.

So be like the bee:

Consistent in your work.

Steady in your habits.

Generous with the growth that overflows from you.

Discipline becomes resilience.

Resilience becomes change.

And change is the first step toward becoming the new you.

But here's the funny thing about becoming:

It doesn't just happen in nature. It happens in the kitchen, too. Because the recipe for growth isn't that different from the recipe for a meatball.

The First Meatball

Once upon a time, there was a meatball.

But before he was a meatball, he was just ground chuck — potential with no purpose. Then someone decided Chuck needed a friend. Breadcrumbs showed up. Breadcrumbs needed someone to hold onto, so eggs joined the party. Eggs needed chemistry, so salt stepped in. Chemistry needed heat, so pepper brought the fire.

All those ingredients sat there, waiting.

Nothing changed… until someone finally reached in and mixed them.

In that moment, the recipe for a meatball was born.

Now imagine if that person never experimented, never played, never imagined combining those ingredients.

Would we have had *Lady and the Tramp*? Would noodles have ever met their soulmate? Probably not.

So here's the truth:

Don't leave the noodles without the meatballs.

Don't stay raw ground chuck when you're one good mix away from becoming something whole.

Creation starts with a thought of growth.

Growing becomes repetition.

Repetition becomes discipline.

Discipline becomes resilience.

Resilience becomes change.

And change is the first step toward becoming the new you.

A meatball needs ingredients.

Your brain needs repetition and intention.

That's the recipe that sparks neuroplasticity.

The Science of Neuroplasticity

Neuroscientist Andrew Huberman explains that neuroplasticity doesn't end in your twenties — it simply becomes gated. After about age twenty-five, the brain still changes. Still, it requires specific triggers, such as norepinephrine and acetylcholine, which factors like caffeine, intense effort, or high-intensity movement can release. His work was the first place I learned this, and it completely reframed how I think about adult learning.

Neural plasticity is your brain's ability to create new neural pathways by taking new actions and exposing yourself to new experiences. For those of us over the age of 25, it helps to be intentional as Huberman suggests. Every time you try something unfamiliar — tasting a new vegetable, jumping rope, lifting a slam ball, climbing a rope, meeting someone new — your brain begins wiring new connections.

So the next time you pick up a book and want to be intentional, prime your brain first. Do a quick HIIT workout. Take a five-minute cold shower or an ice bath. Sip some coffee. Whatever wakes you up and sharpens your focus.

Shift your state on purpose.

Change your mindset on purpose.

Be intentional — and give your brain the spark it needs to grow new neural pathways.

Maybe you'll hold onto the words a little longer. Maybe the ideas will stick a little deeper. Because every time you read with intention, you're teaching your brain to pay attention.

Even doing something familiar in a slightly different way creates a new stimulus, which forces the brain to adapt. And when you repeat that new stimulus over and over, those pathways strengthen. They don't form overnight. They take time, repetition, and consistency to grow into something solid.

That's neural plasticity:

INTENTION → NEW ACTIONS → NEW PATHWAYS → NEW IDENTITY.

Neuroscience shows that the brain begins forming new synaptic connections immediately when exposed to a new stimulus. This is the first spark of neuroplasticity. But those connections are weak at first — like a dirt trail in the woods.

With repetition, the brain strengthens those pathways through a process called long-term potentiation (LTP), which makes the signal travel faster and more reliably. Over days and weeks, repeated activation leads to structural changes — more dendrites, stronger synapses, and eventually myelination, the fatty insulation that turns a skill from "new and awkward" into "automatic and smooth."

This is why repetition matters.

This is why practice works.

This is why the Meatball Parable is biologically true.

Harvard Medical School notes that the brain rewires itself by forming new neural connections in response to new experiences and repeated practice.

Activation energy is the spark that starts the pulse. It's the moment the brain "turns on the light switch" and a behavior begins. Just like when you reach for a glass, your brain sends a signal down a nerve, powered by ATP, and that signal tells your muscles to move. That tiny burst of energy is what gets everything going.

Activation energy is the same thing that gets you to take the first step toward change. It's the energy required to start the action — the mix, the stir, the first thought, the first rep. Once the action begins, the energy needed to keep going drops. But starting? That's where the spark matters.

In neuroscience, activation energy refers to the **threshold** a neuron must reach before it fires. A nerve cell sits quietly until enough electrical charge builds up. Once it hits that threshold, it sends a pulse — an action potential — down the nerve. That pulse is powered by ATP, the same energy molecule your muscles use to move.

This is the biological version of "getting started."

You need enough energy to cross the threshold.

Once you cross it, the signal fires automatically.

That's activation energy:

The spark that starts the behavior.

Harvard Medical School explains that neurons fire only when they reach a specific activation threshold, and that ATP provides the energy needed for those electrical signals to travel. What is activation energy?

Think back to the ingredient list of the meatball: ground chuck, breadcrumbs, eggs, salt, and pepper. Each item sitting there on its own does nothing. It's just potential — a behavior waiting at the threshold. If the chef never mixes them, they sit there forever, full of possibility but never becoming anything.

But the moment the chef mixes the ingredients, the action potential fires. The pulse. The spark. The signal that says, "Go." And the mixing begins. That's the first meatball — the first activation of a new pathway.

It's the same thing that happens the first time you pick up a pen or pencil and try to write. Your handwriting might be sloppy. The meatball might be dry, too salty, bland, too wet, or overcooked. The perfect meatball isn't the ingredient list — those are just the starting conditions—the first action potential in a long line of pulses.

Each spark strengthens the path.

Each repetition refines the recipe.

Each attempt makes the meatball tastier.

Each time you write, your handwriting gets cleaner.

That's how neural pathways form.

That's how identity forms.

That's how the meatball becomes the meatball.

Repetition strengthens neural pathways because each time you perform the same task, you reinforce the connections. You lay down more insulation around the nerve cell, and the more insulated that pathway becomes, the faster the signal travels.

Imagine a road — just a grassy trail through the woods. Trees, rocks, roots everywhere. Hard to walk. Harder to run. That's what a brand-new habit feels like.

Now imagine someone coming through with an axe, clearing the trees that block the way. Suddenly, the path is easier to travel. That's what happens the second time you do a task — you remember what you're doing, you kind of remember how to move your body. You're laying down the first layer of insulation.

But it's still not the dominant path yet.

Because your brain already has a **paved highway** — the old habit. Painted lines, guardrails, signs, smooth asphalt. It's easy. It's familiar. It's fast. And your brain loves fast.

So sometimes you take the old road even when you don't want to.

Not because it's better — but because it's easier.

That's why repetition matters.

Each new attempt is like bringing in an engineer with equipment:

Removing rocks.

Clearing trees.

Widening the trail.

Laying gravel.

Tamping it down.

Paving it.

Painting the lines.

Putting up signs.

And one day, the new road becomes the obvious road.

The preferred road.

The automatic road.

That's myelination.

That's habit formation.

That's identity formation.

Once you choose a new path — a new road, a new direction, a new task, a new skill, a new hobby, a new recipe — you ignite a brand-new neural pathway. That's neuroplasticity. And with repetition, consistency, and practice, you're well on your way to becoming the new you.

Understanding the science is powerful, but it only matters if you use it. Neuroplasticity isn't just a concept — it's a tool. And the moment you apply it to your real life, everything changes.

Real-World Example

Let's say you want to start running, lifting weights, and eating better.

Right now, you walk two to three times a week. You eat out several times a week and grab fast food often. You own dumbbells, but you don't use them consistently.
Start with your why. Then choose the goal that matters most right now.

You choose running.

So instead of walking the whole time, you begin walk-running. Run 50 yards, walk 100. Do that for 45 minutes, two to three times a week for two weeks.

Then run 100 yards, walk 100. Do that for two more weeks.

Gradually, you run longer and walk less. Before you know it, you're running a mile.

Every step along the way, you've been strengthening neural pathways — building the habit of running from the inside out.

Then you apply the same approach to lifting. Then to eating. Layer the habits slowly, and you'll be surprised at how quickly they become part of you.

Small reps. Consistent reps. Intentional reps. That's how a new identity forms.

Application To Your Life

It only applies if you have **intention**.

Without intention, you're just drifting — walking through your days without creating any real change.

Repetition in everyday life depends on your goal.

But at its core, repetition is simply this:

Doing something on purpose, over and over, until it becomes part of you.

For me, that looks like strength training.

Every day is different — legs on Monday, chest on another, shoulders on another.

Some days it's heavyweight.

Some days it's lightweight.

Some days it's a mix of running, biking, or whatever keeps it fun.

The point isn't the perfect plan.

The point is the **repeated effort**.

Every rep provides a stimulus.

Every stimulus sharpens a skill.

Every skill becomes more natural.

And eventually, the movement becomes second nature.

That's habit formation.

That's rewiring.

That's neuroplasticity in real time.

You see changes in your body.

Changes in your strength.

Changes in your coordination.

Changes in how you move, how you feel, how you show up.

The more you practice the movement the way it's meant to be done, the more your fine motor skills fire in sync.

Your body learns.

Your brain learns.

Your identity learns.

Whatever you want to become — a lifter, a runner, a biker, a cook, a writer — it all comes down to the same formula:

INTENTION → REPETITION → PATHWAYS → IDENTITY

Repeat it daily.

Repeat it differently.

Repeat it in ways that stay fun.

Repeat it until it becomes who you are.

Find your why.

Find your purpose.

Find your goal.

And get on with it.

Because the only person holding you back is you.

Understanding how neuroplasticity works is one thing. Seeing it show up in your everyday life is another.

And one of the clearest real-world examples of this kind of growth comes from…

That's how this science shows up in your real life — through the habits you repeat, the choices you make, and the identity you're building. Now it's your turn to look inward and see where this applies to you.

Reflection Questions

1. When you imagine the person you want to become, what traits or ingredients belong in that version of you? Which ones are missing from your current recipe?

2. Which ingredient will you focus on first? What habits will help you turn that trait into second nature?

3. What is your activation energy — your spark, your why? What's the reason you're pushing for change? Write it down and keep it close.

4. What repeated actions will help you blend your new traits into your life? Will you mix slowly, blend at high speed, or knead the dough patiently and let it rise — the same way you'll rise as these traits settle into you?

5. Once your ingredients have mixed, proofed, and become part of your identity, how does that shift the way you see yourself? What changes in your mindset?

By now, you've reflected on your habits, your wiring, and your growth.

So let's shift gears.

Because sometimes the clearest lessons about becoming come from the most unlikely places — like a coyote with a mail-order addiction, a hunter who never hits his target, and a rooster who talks too much.

3

Wile E., Elmer, and Foghorn – Repetition vs Wisdom

Sometimes in life, we chase the best version of ourselves with everything we've got — and somehow, we still can't catch it. Not because it's impossible, but because we're not thinking deeply enough. We're not reflecting. We're not looking inward with honesty and precision.

Only when we look closely at who we are and who we want to become do we finally sharpen the target. Only then can we put a bull's-eye on what needs to change.

I've always loved cartoons. I watched them endlessly as a kid — the reruns, the loops, the same scenes over and over. And now, decades later, I see something I never noticed back then:

Those cartoons were teaching repetition long before I ever learned the word neuroplasticity.

This book is about that exact thing — repetition, intention, and taking action with purpose. Because when we want to grow, we have to look at our mistakes, understand them, and decide how to move forward.

So take a look at the Road Runner, Wile E. Coyote, and all the other characters I grew up watching. Forty years later, I see them differently. I see myself in them. I see all of us in them.

But here's the problem: most of us chase our future selves like we're trying to catch Speedy Gonzales. Or worse — like we're Wile E. Coyote chasing the Road Runner. And what did Wile E. do every single time?

He made a plan.

Did the plan work?

Absolutely not.

But have you ever wondered *why* it never worked?

Because Wile E. never refined anything.

He never stuck with one trap long enough to improve it.

He just moved on to the next ACME gadget like a kid with a short attention span and a credit card.

So, if Wiley had taken one idea — just one — and refined it, repeated it, improved it, and perfected it… who knows? Maybe he would've finally caught the Beeper. We'll never know.

But here's what we *do* know:

If you want to catch your future self, you have to finish the first thing you're working on before sprinting to the second, the third, or the fifteenth. Otherwise, you're just Wile E. in a never-ending loop of almost-catching, almost-becoming, almost-changing.

So stop chasing your goals like a cartoon.

Execute them with the precision of Elmer Fudd and the wisdom of Foghorn Leghorn.

Elmer had the repetition — he chased Bugs every single day.

Foghorn had the wisdom — loud, ridiculous, but somehow always right.

Elmer needed Foghorn's brain.

Foghorn needed Elmer's persistence.

Together, they would've been unstoppable.

Wile E. had repetition.

Foghorn had wisdom.

Elmer had persistence.

But none of them had all three.

So what wisdom are *you* missing?

That's why they stayed stuck — and why you don't have to.

How can you outsmart the Beeper, Bugs Bunny, and — most importantly — yourself?

It all starts with intention.

And it grows with repetition.

Repetition gives you movement.

Wisdom gives you direction.

But identity — who you believe you are — gives you power.

And that's where the next story begins.

The Power Within

When you watch He-Man and the Power of Grayskull, it looks like a story about strength — but it's really a growth story.

Before he ever became He-Man, Prince Adam wasn't strong.

He wasn't confident.

He wasn't the hero everyone expected him to be.

He had a reputation he didn't feel big enough to carry. He didn't fit the mold he was "supposed" to fit. And that's the part people forget: he wasn't inherently powerful. He didn't start strong.

Everything changed the moment he lifted the sword, trusted the Power of Grayskull, and transformed.

He became strong only after he believed.

The power didn't show up first — the trust did.

Just like us.

We all grow up with expectations — some we choose, some are chosen for us. Some we want, some we never asked for.

Prince Adam didn't choose the responsibility. He was chosen.

But here's the truth:

You can be chosen too — the moment you choose yourself.

He-Man didn't become powerful because of a sword.

The sword was just the symbol.

The real power was effort.

The real power was belief.

The real power lay in stepping outside his comfort zone and becoming the version of himself he kept avoiding.

And that's the lesson.

Every one of us has our own "Power of Grayskull."

It doesn't matter what you call it.

It doesn't matter where it comes from.

What matters is that it's already inside you — waiting for effort, intention, and belief to wake it up.

You don't need a sword.

You need to choose yourself.

Belief is the spark that starts the transformation.

But once the spark is lit, growth becomes a pattern — something you build day after day.

And that's where the next story begins.

Rising

"Rising"

There's something about looking into the sunrise that reminds me how much of life is pattern.

The sun rises because it follows its pattern.

And people rise the same way — not all at once, not on command, but when their patterns finally support the person they're trying to become.

Growth isn't just about habits.

It's thoughts, emotions, and the connections we carry with us.

Some connections are fragmented and pull us apart.

Some are solid and hold us steady.

Some are misplaced and confuse the direction we're trying to go.

And all of them shape how we show up in the world.

When we feel supported, showing up is easier.

When we feel alone, showing up becomes heavier.

But the real turning point — the moment you start becoming who you're meant to be — is when you show up, whether you're supported or not.

Not because it's easy.

Not because it's comfortable.

But because the pattern inside you has changed.

Rising isn't an event.

It's a pattern you build.

And once it's built, you rise the same way the sun does — consistently, quietly, and without asking permission.

Patterns help you rise.

But not every pattern is built in comfort.

Some of the strongest ones are forged in moments you would

never choose — the ones that hurt, scar, and shape you in ways you don't understand until years later.

And that's where the next story comes in.

The Concrete Burns

When I was in the Air Force, I missed a safety briefing before a concrete job. I didn't think much of it at the time. I was helping, knee-deep in wet concrete, doing what needed to be done.

Hours later, I learned what concrete can do to skin.

Both of my legs burned where the blousing straps held the concrete against my ankles. The chemical burn left deep scars — an inch and a half wide on each side —, and it took a long time to heal. I had to go to the hospital, but even after that, they still made me do PT.

Every time I ran, the scabs tore open.

Every step stung.

Every mile felt like the skin was splitting again.

It wasn't inspiring.

It wasn't motivating.

It was just painful.

But something else was happening underneath the pain — something I didn't understand back then.

My brain was learning.

Every painful step was a signal firing down a pathway I had never used before. A pathway that said, "You can keep going even when it hurts." Not in a reckless way. Not in a macho way. In a disciplined way.

That experience didn't turn me into the person I am now. But it planted the first seed of discipline — the kind that grows slowly, quietly, and through repetition.

Neuroplasticity isn't always formed by inspiring moments. Sometimes it's formed by the moments you would never choose — the ones that scar you, literally and mentally, but also teach your brain a new pattern:

"I can endure. I can adapt. I can keep moving."

Those scars on my ankles aren't reminders of pain.

They're reminders of the first time my brain rewired itself toward discipline.

Pain taught me discipline long before I understood why it worked.

Years later, I learned the science behind it — the biology that explains how moments like that reshape the brain and build the patterns we carry for life.

Science of Intention

When you look back at the stories of Elmer Fudd, Bugs Bunny, and Foghorn Leghorn, one thing becomes obvious: intention. But intention alone isn't enough. "Neurons that fire together wire together." — Hebbian Principle (1949) Sometimes we have the best intentions, but not the right intention — and the right intention requires understanding what's happening inside us.

"Attention is the gateway to neuroplasticity." — Cognitive Neuroscience Principle. As we get older, intention needs a precursor. A spark. Something that wakes up the brain and prepares it to grow. Because growth isn't just emotional or motivational — it's biological. It's chemical. It's neuroplasticity.

And neuroplasticity needs fuel.

Two chemicals in particular — acetylcholine and norepinephrine — act like the ignition switch for learning. They sharpen focus, increase alertness, and prime the brain to build new neural pathways. Without them, intention stalls. With them, intention becomes action.

So before you try to learn something new — a skill, a job, a habit, a mindset — give your brain the spark it needs.

Take a cold shower.

Do a quick HIIT workout.

Drink some coffee or tea.

Shock your system just enough to wake up those chemicals.

That's the precursor.

That's the ignition.

That's the moment intention becomes possible.

Because once those chemicals are active, your actions start to matter. Your reps start to count. Your brain begins laying down the first layer of a new pathway — and every repetition strengthens it. Do it again and again and again, and the road you're paving becomes smoother, faster, and eventually automatic.

And when that happens, the road you once struggled to walk becomes a road you can fly on.

Science Application: Why We Chase, Why We Quit, and Why Repetition Wins

Before we talk about diets, goals, or chasing the future version of ourselves, we have to understand what's happening inside the brain long before we ever take action.
Most people don't fail because they're lazy.

They fail because their **brains are wired to chase novelty instead of mastery**.

1. The Brain Loves the Chase More Than the Goal

The dopamine system — the brain's motivation engine — fires strongest during **anticipation**, not achievement.

That means:

Dreaming about the goal feels exciting.

Planning feels productive.

imagining the future self feels rewarding

But the moment the work becomes repetitive, dopamine drops.

The brain starts whispering:

"Maybe there's a faster way."

"Maybe there's a better plan."

"Maybe you should try something new."

That's the Wile E. Coyote loop — chasing, switching, restarting, never refining.

2. Intention Without Attention Doesn't Create Change

Neuroscience shows that **attention is the gateway to neuroplasticity**.

You can have the best intentions in the world, but if your attention is scattered — if you're jumping from plan to plan — the brain never gets enough repetition to build a new pathway.

Intention sets the direction.

Attention builds the road.

3. Neuroplasticity Needs Repetition, Not Perfection

Every new skill, habit, or identity begins the same way:

Thought → Action → Repetition → Identity

The *thought* sparks the pathway.

The *action* strengthens it.

The *repetition* wires it.

The *identity* emerges from it.

This is why Prince Adam didn't become He-Man until he believed.

Belief activates intention.

Intention activates repetition.

Repetition activates identity.

The sword was just the symbol.

The real power was the pattern.

4. Pain Teaches the Brain Too

Not all neuroplasticity comes from inspiration.

Some of it comes from the moments we would never choose — like your concrete burns.

Pain creates a different kind of learning:

Endurance.

Discipline.

Resilience.

The ability to keep moving even when it hurts.

Those pathways are built the same way as any other — through repetition.

Every painful step was your brain saying:

"I can adapt. I can endure. I can keep going."

That's neuroplasticity in its rawest form.

5. Patterns Create Identity

The sun rises because it follows its pattern.
People rise the same way.

When your patterns change:

Your thoughts change.

Your emotions change.

Your behaviors change.

Your identity changes.

Rising isn't a moment.

It's a pattern you build.

And once the pattern is built, you rise the same way the sun does — consistently, quietly, without asking permission.

6. Why We Quit Too Early

The brain is wired to prefer:

Novelty over repetition.

Excitement over consistency.

Anticipation over follow-through.

That's why people jump on diets.

That's why they chase new plans.

That's why they restart instead of refining.

Not because they're weak — but because their brain hasn't built the pathway yet.

7. The Real Science of Change

Change happens when:

Intention is clear.

Attention is focused.

Repetition is consistent.

Chemistry is activated.

Acetylcholine sharpens focus.

Norepinephrine increases alertness.

Repetition strengthens pathways.

Identity emerges from the pattern.

This is the biology behind becoming.

This is the science behind discipline.

This is why the future version of you stays out of reach until you stop chasing like a cartoon character and start building like an artisan.

Because once the pathway is built, everything changes.

Understanding the science explains *how* change happens.

But to see why we struggle — and why repetition matters — we have to look at how this plays out in real life.

And nowhere is that clearer than in the way people approach dieting.

Real-World Example: The Diet Carousel

Most people don't fail because they pick the "wrong" diet. They fail because they keep switching diets.

In the real world, this is what happens:

Someone decides they're finally ready to change. They pick a diet — keto, paleo, low-fat, intermittent fasting, whatever is trending that week. For the first few days, they're perfect. They track every calorie, measure every bite, and follow every rule.

And then the scale doesn't move fast enough.

Maybe they expected three pounds the first week and only lost one.

Maybe they expected to feel different by day four and… nothing.

Maybe they did everything "right" and still didn't see the version of themselves they were chasing.

So they quit.

And the moment they quit, they start looking for the next diet — the one that will finally "work."

This becomes a loop: try → expect fast results → get disappointed → quit → repeat.

It's not a lack of knowledge.

It's not a lack of effort.

It's the disappointment cycle.

The truth is simpler than the diet carousel.

Most people don't need a new diet.

They need a simple system they can actually stick to.

Something like:

Eat real food.

Hit the right amount of protein.

Get enough fat to stay satisfied.

Keep carbs mostly to fiber-rich sources.

That's it.

Not glamorous. Not trendy. Not viral.

But it works — every time, for everybody, in every decade.

Why people still chase diets

Because they're not just chasing weight loss.

They're chasing a version of themselves they want to become.

And when the results don't show up fast enough, they assume the diet is broken — not the timeline in their head.

So they jump to the next plan.

And the next.

And the next.

Never long enough to see what consistency could have done.

The real solution

Whatever approach you choose, stick with it long enough to let it work.

Get with a dietitian.

Find the right macro targets for your body.

Eat real food.

Repeat.

Not for three days.

Not for three weeks.

But long enough to break the disappointment cycle.

That's when everything changes.

The diet carousel is just one example.

But the truth is, this pattern shows up everywhere — in every goal, every habit, every version of yourself you're trying to build.

And that's where the real application begins.

Real Life Application

Nothing in the real world comes easy. Everything you want requires sticking with the process long enough for the results to show up. Whether it's being consistent with your diet, studying for school, learning a new job, practicing guitar, or building any other skill, the rule never changes:

The key is consistency.

If you stick with the process long enough, you will see results. But if you give up too early, you'll spend your life chasing goals the way Wile E. Coyote chases the Road Runner — always running, always trying, but never staying on one path long enough to catch what you're after.

Sticking with something day after day eventually builds wisdom. At first, it feels slow, frustrating, and unrewarding. But if you keep showing up, something changes. You begin to understand what you're doing. You start seeing patterns. You start making fewer mistakes. You begin to build momentum.

It's like teaming up with your own inner Foghorn Leghorn — the voice of experience that finally says, "I say, I say, stick with it long enough, and you'll get exactly what you came for."

Consistency turns effort into skill.

Skill turns into confidence.

Confidence turns into results.

Whatever you're trying to learn or improve — your diet, your job, your guitar playing, your education, or your fitness — the truth is simple:

Wile E. Coyote never catches the Road Runner because he's always looking for the next gadget, the next shortcut, the next perfect plan.

Success usually comes from something much less exciting:

Doing the same useful things long enough for them to work.

That's when everything changes.

That's how these patterns show up in the real world — in diets, goals, habits, and every version of yourself you're trying to build. Now it's your turn to look inward and see where these patterns are shaping your own becoming.

Reflection Questions

1. Name a time you finished what you started.

What did it feel like to follow through? What changed in you afterward?

2. Name a time you gave up on a goal.

Why did you stop? What would you do differently now with the mindset you have today?

3. Name a time you worked through something difficult and came out stronger.

What was the challenge, and how did you feel afterward?

4. Have you ever put intention before starting something new?

If not, how would you use intention now to begin something with purpose?

5. How do you use what you know to stay persistent and build discipline?

What tools, habits, or mindsets help you stay consistent?

Repetition and wisdom fit together like Foghorn Leghorn hollering at Elmer Fudd. Now it's time to twist the lid off complacency and let the cucumber of your old habits transform into a crisp, new pickle of possibility.

4

The Pickle Parable – Time + Transformation

Sometimes in life, we struggle with who we want to become — not because we don't want to change, but because we don't know how to change. We've been ourselves our whole lives. We've only ever seen the world from inside our own skin. We've never stepped outside ourselves long enough to see what others see.

And because of that, we don't always reflect.

We don't always listen.

We don't always open ourselves to the kind of feedback that could actually help us grow.

But then one day, someone gives us a piece of constructive criticism — not to tear us down, but to show us something we never noticed. And for the first time, we pause. We reflect. We ask ourselves who we really are… and who we actually want to become.

That's when we realize something important:

Sometimes we start in life like a cucumber.

We don't know we can be anything else.

We don't know if we can add salt, spice, or sweetness.

We don't know we can transform.

We only ever saw ourselves as what we were — not what we could become.

And that leads me to the cucumber.

A long time ago, there was a cucumber that thought it was the coolest thing in the garden. He didn't know what he was supposed to be. Some people called him a vegetable. Some insisted he was a fruit. Scientifically? Botanically? He had no clue. He was confused, lost somewhere between salad and science.

Then someone came along and sparked a transformation with chemistry again.

They sliced him.

They bathed him.

Vinegar showed up.

Vinegar needed sweetness.

Sweetness needed salt.

Salt needs balance.

But the most important ingredient — the one the cucumber never expected — was **time**.

Because in time, he became the iconic pickle.

Was he the first pickle ever made?

I don't know. I haven't researched it.

But is he the most famous pickle of all time?

Absolutely.

And guess what?

All it took was time, persistence, and a little bit of cultivating mixed into a jar. The lid sealed the potential. The potential sat still. And when the time was right — when the lid finally came off — stagnation ended, and transformation began.

After the pickle emerged from the jar, he told everyone else not to be so NaCl. And from there, he kept evolving. New flavors. New spices. New jars. And with every new jar came a new lid to pop.

Life doesn't stop at the first change.

Change is inevitable — if you allow it.

Change happens when you have intention.

Change happens when you take the first step.

So get out there.

Start.

"The amygdala is the brain's threat detector. It reacts before we are even aware of the danger." —Joseph LeDoux, NYU Center for Neural Science.

The pickle showed us how transformation happens over time. But not all growth is loud or dramatic. Some of it begins quietly — deep beneath the surface — long before anyone can see it.

A Seed that breaks the soil

A seed breaks the soil because something inside it refuses to stay small.

It reaches for the sun long before it understands what the sun even is.

Day after day, it rises — slow, steady, patient — until it becomes the thing it was meant to be.

A plant has a season.

It grows, it blooms, it gives what it can, and then its cycle ends.

Its usefulness fades, its leaves fall, and the only thing that continues is the seed it leaves behind.

But we are not plants.

We go through cycles too — seasons of effort, seasons of loss, seasons of rebuilding.

And sometimes a cycle ends.

But unlike the plant, we don't start over from nothing.

We don't return to the seed.

We don't lose everything we've built.

We regroup.

We rethink.

We re-analyze what we truly want.

And if the desire is still alive — if the hunger is still there — we rise again.

Every cycle leaves us with more than we had before:
more wisdom, more clarity, more resilience, more truth about who we are and who we're becoming.

A plant grows until nature tells it to stop.

We grow until we decide to stop.

And if we choose not to stop, the amount of growth available to us is infinite.

That's the difference.

That's the power.

That's the freedom we have that no plant ever will.

So instead of planting something cute, plant a version of yourself, changing something you've always wanted to change. Plant the future you — the you that you've imagined a hundred times but never given the chance to break through. Somewhere along the way, you set the seed aside and walked away from the person you were becoming.

Now is your chance to pick it back up and give it the light it needs.

So take the next step.

Write down your change.

Write down what you want to grow into.

Once you write it down, you've planted your first seed — the future version of you, ten steps ahead, waiting for you to catch up.

But even when growth begins, it doesn't always get the chance to flourish. Sometimes the problem isn't the seed at all — it's what tries to stop it from rising.

The Deer and the Grapevine

A grapevine always tries to grow.

It doesn't need to be taught.

It doesn't need to be motivated.

Growth is simply what it was made to do.

But in the garden, the deer come early.

They don't wait for the vine to flourish.

They don't wait for fruit to appear.

They eat it while it's still inches out of the ground — before it ever has a chance.

Every one of us has a garden like that.

Something inside us that wants to grow.

Something that wants to bear fruit.

Something that was designed to flourish.

And every one of us has a deer.

Something that eats our progress before it matures.

Fear.

Stress.

Old habits.

People who drain us.

Distractions that nibble away at our momentum.

The problem isn't the vine.

The problem is what's feeding on it.

If you want your grapes to grow, you don't yell at the vine.

You don't blame the soil.

You don't wait for better weather.

You build a wall around the deer.

You identify the thing that keeps eating your growth, and you protect the part of you that's trying to rise.

Because once the deer is kept out, the vine doesn't need encouragement.

It grows on its own.

It always has.

And even when nothing is actively stopping us, we still face another challenge — the slow leak of daily life, the quiet drain that pulls us down without us noticing.

The Balloon That Leaked

Imagine you're filling balloons for a party.

Some balloons get a quick breath of air.

Some get helium so they float higher.

Some get High-Float so they last longer.

But no matter how carefully you fill them, every balloon eventually does the same thing:

It slowly leaks.

It sinks.

It softens.

It loses its lift.

And people do this too.

We take on the world — one task, one responsibility, one expectation at a time.

We fill ourselves with big goals, small goals, new habits, old habits, and everything in between.

Some days, the air we add lifts us.

Some days it weighs us down.

Some days, we overfill ourselves without realizing it.

And just like a balloon stretched too thin, we leak.

Not all at once.

Not dramatically.

Just slowly… quietly… steadily.

The key isn't to stay perfectly full.

The key is to **fill yourself with the right amount each day** — not too much, not too little.

A little effort.

A little growth.

A little pressure.

Just enough to rise.

Because when you try to pump yourself full of everything at once — every task, every goal, every expectation — you don't fly higher.

You pop.

But when you add just enough air each day — one habit, one step, one small win — you stay lifted.

You stay steady.

You stay becoming.

Don't stay trapped inside a sagging, half-deflated balloon of old expectations.

Give yourself the right amount of air today.

Just enough to rise again.

These stories aren't just metaphors. There's a real, biological reason we struggle to grow, to rise, and to stay lifted. The answer lives inside the brain.

The Science of What's Really Happening Inside the Pickle Jar

"The amygdala is the brain's threat detector. It reacts before we are even aware of the danger." — Joseph LeDoux, NYU Center for Neural Science.

When we stay "cucumbers," it's not because we're lazy or broken. It's because of what's happening inside the brain. We live our entire lives inside our own minds, seeing the world only from our perspective. That creates a kind of glass jar — familiar, comfortable, sealed tight — and we don't even realize we put the lid on ourselves.

Inside that jar are all the memories, beliefs, habits, and neural pathways we built growing up. They're strong — incredibly strong — because they were designed to keep us safe, fed, accepted, and loved. Those pathways come from family, culture, environment, and experience. And with culture comes pride. With pride comes rigidity. And with rigidity comes resistance to change.

Not because we're stubborn.

But because our brain is protecting us.

That protection comes from the amygdala — the part of the brain responsible for fear, threat detection, and survival. It's the fight-flight-freeze center. It wants us to stay in familiar territory. It wants us to avoid risk. It wants us to keep the lid on the jar. The amygdala doesn't care about growth. It cares about safety. It cares about familiarity. It cares about keeping you exactly where you are, even if that's not where you want to be.

"The prefrontal cortex allows us to reflect, plan, and override automatic responses." — Harvard Medical School.

But something powerful happens when we reflect — truly reflect.

When we pause, question, and look inward with honesty, another part of the brain steps in: the prefrontal cortex.

This is the part of the brain that reasons.

The part that evaluates.

The part that sees possibilities instead of threats.

It's the Buddha of the brain — calm, steady, wise.

It's the Dalai Lama of decision-making — patient, intentional, grounded.

It's the river that flows and adapts — not the dam that holds everything back.

Reflection quiets the amygdala.

Reflection activates the prefrontal cortex.

Reflection opens the jar's lid.

The moment you reflect, you create space between stimulus and response. You create a gap wide enough for choice. You create a moment where you can see yourself not as you've always been, but as you could become.

"Executive functions enable us to pause, think, and choose a response instead of reacting automatically." — American Psychological Association.

This is the moment the lid loosens.

This is the moment the jar opens.

This is the moment the cucumber realizes it doesn't have to stay a cucumber.

Because once you understand what's happening inside your brain — once you see the amygdala trying to protect you and the prefrontal cortex trying to grow you — you're no longer trapped by old wiring. You're no longer sealed inside the version of yourself you've always been.

You gain the ability — and the responsibility — to grow.

You gain the freedom to add salt, spice, sweetness, and time.

You gain the courage to step out of the jar.

You gain the clarity to become the pickle — the transformed version of yourself you never knew you could be.

And this shows up in everyday life more than we realize — especially in the moments when someone tries to help us grow.

Real-World Example

In the real world, listening is harder than it sounds. When someone gives us feedback or tries to help us improve, we often get defensive — not because we don't want to change, but because our amygdala is trying to keep us safe. A simple comment can feel like a threat. A suggestion can feel like an attack. Our defenses rise before we even realize it.

Instead of listening, we start preparing our response. We explain. We justify. We argue in our heads. We react to what we think we heard, or what we're afraid they meant, instead of what was actually said.

When the goal of a conversation is growth, the key is to slow down and truly listen. Pause. Reflect. Ask yourself how the message might apply to you. Listen deeply. Listen as you mean it. Listen all the way through before acting on your assumptions. There is a big difference between reacting to your first interpretation and responding to what was truly spoken.

The more you practice that kind of listening, the more wisdom you'll find in conversations that used to feel threatening.

When you understand what's happening inside your brain, you can finally apply it to your life with clarity and intention.

Application to Your Life

A beautiful thing happens when you accept feedback with a growth mindset. You permit yourself to see where you can improve, or to consider a different way of thinking from someone else's perspective. Real transformation happens when you can take your perspective and someone else's perspective and combine them into one clearer vision.

We can't see ourselves the way others see us, but we can consider their perception and their recommendations.

There is nothing wrong with looking at something from another angle. When you reflect honestly and decide whether those recommendations fit, that's when real change begins.

Growth doesn't come from defending who you already are — it comes from being open to who you could become.

Just like the cucumber, we don't transform overnight. We grow when we allow new experiences, new perspectives, and new lessons to sit with us long enough to change us.

Sometimes the feedback we resist most is the very ingredient we needed to become something more.

The cucumber became a pickle because it was willing to sit in the process long enough to be transformed.

Growth works the same way.

The feedback.

The reflection.

The discomfort.

The time.

Those are often the ingredients that help us become the person we're meant to be.

Now it's your turn to look inward and explore how these ideas show up in your own becoming.

Reflection Questions:

1. How do you seek feedback when you want to grow?
Do you ask directly? Do you avoid it? Do you only accept feedback from certain people?

2. Do you live with a growth mindset, or do you accept life exactly as it is?

Where do you see yourself resisting change? Where do you embrace it?

3. Name a time you stepped outside your comfort zone.
What pushed you? What scared you? What did you learn about yourself?

4. How do you know which "spices" to add to your jar to take the lid off?

What habits, influences, or mindsets help you transform? Which ones hold you back?

5. What does the best version of you look like?
Describe them clearly — their habits, their mindset, their discipline, their energy!

You don't always know the exact moment you're ready to grow. Sometimes the shift begins quietly — long before you notice it. And when it finally arrives, it doesn't come with fireworks. It comes as a feeling, a memory, a whisper from somewhere deep inside you.

5

The Breeze + Caterpillar-Readiness

These moments — the ones that stir something old inside us — are often the first signs that change is coming. And that brings me to the story of the breeze and the caterpillar.

Sometimes a smell, a warmth, a sudden chill, or the way the wind brushes against our skin slips into us in a way we can't explain. It drifts through us as a whisper from a place we forgot existed. And in that moment, something stirs — something we don't quite remember, something we tucked away deep inside our mind long ago.

We don't choose when these memories return.

They come back only when the time is right.

Only when the conditions are perfect.

Only when we're finally ready to feel them again.

And when they do return, they open inside us like a door we didn't know was locked. The memory arrives exactly as it was the first time — the first time we heard it, the first time we saw it, the first time we felt it, smelled it, touched it. It comes back whole, untouched, waiting for us.

And sometimes, it's only in that moment — when the forgotten becomes familiar again — that our cocoon finally cracks open. Only then do we step out, wings unfolding, transformed into the newest and best version of ourselves.

And that brings me to the story of the breeze and the caterpillar.

In the early morning, there was a breeze — and in that breeze was a thought. Sometimes our thoughts blow away like that, drifting off into the wind and never returning. Don't let your goals be carried off the same way.

And so it began.

Those thoughts floated into the air, becoming the first sparks of readiness. Because sometimes when we want to change, we're not ready yet — and that's okay.

Not everything lines up like the meatball, Elmer, Foghorn, and the pickle. Some changes take days. Some take months. Some take years.

Which brings me to the caterpillar.

For a caterpillar to grow, it has to feed. And when it feeds, it grows. And once it grows enough, a cascade of hormones tells it to stop eating, shed its shell, and return to the wind — to gather the thoughts it once lost and bring them back home.

Sometimes your thought needs fuel.

It needs time.

It needs the right ingredients.

It needs the right person, the right job, the right book, the right experience.

And when all of that finally lines up — when you've fed the thought long enough — you enter your cocoon. You sit by yourself. You transform in the quiet.

And then, when the time is right, you emerge.

Not who you were.

But as the new version of yourself.

But even when transformation begins, it doesn't happen all at once. Growth has a pace, and that pace matters — which leads to another story.

The Long Race

When you slow down long enough to really look at the things you want, you start to realize something: life moves better at a steady pace. "Slow and steady wins the race" isn't just a cliché — it fits almost everything. It fits your goals. It fits the things you hope for. It fits friendships.

Some friendships matter more than others. Some goals matter more than others. Some things in life are just going to sit higher on your list. But the key is the same in all of them: don't force it.

When you try to force goals, you burn yourself out. You push too hard, too fast, and then you wonder why you're exhausted. The trick is pacing yourself — building momentum slowly, letting it stack, letting it grow. Once you have that momentum, you can keep pushing without breaking yourself.

Friendships work the same way, except you're not building momentum — you're building closeness, trust, and the simple enjoyment of talking. You don't rush that. You don't sprint it. You let it grow at its own speed.

Whatever you're working on — goals, friendships, life — take your time. Pace yourself. Life isn't a sprint. It isn't even a marathon.

It's one long ultramarathon.

And while pace shapes our progress, something else shapes us too — the way our experiences change our inner flavor over time.

Taste & Time

Coffee and I have been together a long time.

At first, it was bitter — sharper than I wanted, harsher than I expected.

But I kept coming back.

Over time, the bitterness softened.

Or maybe I did.

I added warmth, then flavor, then texture.

The cup changed in my hands, and I changed with it.

Sip by sip, morning by morning, I learned something simple:

Coffee isn't the only thing that changes day by day.
We do.

Our taste shifts as our lives shift.

Once we were bitter.

Once we were sour.

Once we were sweet.

And sometimes we cycle through all three in the same season.

We can't control what life hands us —
the heat, the pressure, the unexpected flavors.

But we can control how we respond.

When we practice pausing in the height of the moment, we give ourselves a chance to choose something better.

Our actions can't be taken back.

But our thoughts can be rewoven.

Thread by thread.

Into something that grows us instead of breaks us.

Because just like taste, we are allowed to change.

And sometimes the change is the very thing that saves us.

These shifts aren't random. There's a reason certain moments, tastes, and sensations change us so deeply — and the answer lives inside the brain.

The Science Smell and D.O.E.S

The sense of smell can evoke powerful emotional memories because it has direct connections to the amygdala and hippocampus." — Harvard University, Department of Neurobiology.

Sometimes a smell, a breeze, a shift in temperature, or the warmth of sunlight doesn't just touch our skin — it slips into us. It drifts through us like a quiet messenger, carrying something we don't fully recognize. And suddenly, without warning, we remember something we didn't even know we forgot.

A feeling.

A moment.

A person.

A version of ourselves we left behind.

This isn't imagination.

It's neuroscience.

When a sensory cue hits the brain — especially smell — it travels straight to the amygdala (emotion) and hippocampus (memory). That's why a scent can unlock a memory faster than a photograph ever could.

"Emotionally charged memories are stored more strongly because of the interaction between the amygdala and hippocampus." — National Institutes of Health (NIH)

Inside your brain, memories aren't stored as files. They're stored as neural pathways — networks of emotion, sensation, and meaning. When a cue matches one of those pathways, the brain releases a rush of chemicals that bring the memory back online.

Dopamine — motivation, reward, anticipation.
Oxytocin — bonding, connection, emotional warmth.
Epinephrine — intensity, alertness, emotional imprinting.
Serotonin — mood, stability, well-being.

The chemicals known as **D.O.E.S**. surge through the brain during emotional recall. They act like keys, unlocking memories that have been resting quietly beneath the surface.

They're like keys waiting for the right lock.

A familiar smell.

A forgotten song.

The way the wind hits your face at the exact angle it did when you were young.

These cues activate the brain's emotional centers, and chemicals surge.

That surge is the spark — the light switch — the tiny ignition that wakes up a memory that's been sleeping in the dark.

"Memory retrieval is cue-dependent; the right sensory or emotional trigger can reactivate dormant neural pathways." — American Psychological Association.

The spark travels through the brain like a fuse, lighting up the pathway where that memory has been stored. It's not gone. It's not lost. It's just been dormant, tucked away in a closet inside your mind, waiting for the right moment to be opened again.

And when that closet opens, the memory returns exactly as it was:

The first time you felt it.

The first time you heard it.

The first time you smelled it.

The first time it mattered.

This is why certain moments feel like déjà vu, or like time folding in on itself.

It's not magic.

It's neurochemistry.

It's your brain saying, "You're ready now."

Because when those chemicals surge, they don't just bring back memories — they bring back you. They bring back the parts of you that were waiting to be remembered so you could grow into the next version of yourself.

That spark is the beginning of transformation.
It's the moment the cocoon cracks.

It's the moment the caterpillar realizes it was never meant to stay on the ground.

And this isn't just theory. You can see this same pattern in everyday life, especially when people face big changes.

Real World Example: What Are We Afraid Of?

When thinking about change, many people are afraid to change careers or go back to college later in life. But if we look around, we see countless people who have done exactly that. They went back to school in their thirties, forties, fifties, and beyond. Others started entirely new careers after years of doing something different.

It's not nearly as uncommon as we think.

So what are we really afraid of?

Often, it's our amygdala trying to protect us from uncertainty. Change feels unfamiliar, and unfamiliar things can feel threatening. But change is a natural part of life.

From the day we are born until the day we leave this earth, we are constantly changing. In many ways, we are reborn every single day into a slightly different version of ourselves.

When we accept that growth is a daily process, transformation becomes much less intimidating. Instead of worrying about who we need to become five years from now, we can focus on becoming a little better today.

Sign up for that college class.

Apply for that job you don't feel ready for.

Take the first step toward the goal that keeps calling your name.

Growth happens when we lean forward instead of falling back.

Nature is always moving forward, and we should too. The key is to gather the right ingredients—knowledge, experience, effort, patience, and courage—and allow them to work together inside us.

Just as the caterpillar eventually emerges from its cocoon, we can emerge into a new version of ourselves when the time is right.

Once you understand how memory, emotion, and readiness work together, you can finally apply these ideas to your own growth.

Application To Your Life

We are not always ready for every goal we have, and that is okay. Life moves in seasons. Days become months. Months become years. Years become decades.

The mistake many people make is focusing only on the distant outcome while ignoring the actions available today.

Transformation happens one day at a time.

What you accomplish in a single day may seem small, but those days compound into months, years, and eventually an entirely different life.

Instead of spending your energy thinking about how you want to change, spend it taking action.

Take in the right ingredients.

Learn.

Practice.

Reflect.

Grow.

Focus on the day in front of you and take thoughtful action toward the person you want to become.

That is how transformation begins.

Now it's your turn to explore how these ideas show up in your life and your becoming.

Reflection Questions:

1. What do you do when you feel that familiar trigger rising?

Describe your first reaction — physical, emotional, or mental. Do you pause, avoid, react, or redirect?

2. What do you do to feed your growth?

Do you read, listen to podcasts, watch TED Talks, take classes, journal, or talk to mentors? What actually nourishes you?

3. On days when you feel bitter, sour, sweet, or salty — do you notice it?

And when you do notice it, do you stop and ask yourself why?

4. When you realize you're not growing, how do you respond?

Do you accept it, or do you intentionally work on yourself?

5. Think of a time you tried to grow.
Did you give yourself the right tools? Or did you set yourself up to fail without realizing it?

Growth doesn't always arrive with clarity. Sometimes it begins in the quiet moments — the ones that stir something inside you before you even understand why. And when you follow those moments long enough, they lead you into a new kind of awareness.

6

Learning in the Dark

And sometimes the only way to understand yourself more deeply is to step into the dark and let your other senses rise to meet the moment.

A little bit of different, a little bit of what you're not used to — a little hidden love that slips right through the cracks. Sometimes you don't see it. Sometimes you don't feel it. But sometimes you taste it. And when you taste it, when that rush of emotion hits, it feels like sitting at the edge of the world.

It's the moment you start believing again and trusting again.

Knowing you're on the right path.

Because if you keep going — day after day — following the plan, building the habits, and taking the actions that build them, something shifts. And when you reflect each night on what you did right, what you did okay, and what you want to improve… You stop dwelling. You start designing.

And then one day, peace unfolds. Quietly. Softly. Like a veil lifting.

And when that veil lifts, you become one with yourself. You stop trying to be anything else. You just are. And that's where you've always wanted to be.

So think. Reflect. Watch the world unfold — through your eyes, and through the eyes of others — so you can finally experience life the way it was meant to be experienced.

Sometimes you find yourself standing in darkness —
not because the lights are off, but because your eyes are closed.

You know what you need to do.

Your body knows, too.

But the signal won't fire.

So you breathe.

You focus.

You let your neurons do their job.

You move your arm.

You shift your weight.

You take a step into the dark.

You can't see your surroundings, but you begin to feel them.

The floor beneath your feet.

The air brushes your skin.

The shape of something familiar in your hand.

You've seen this object a thousand times,
but only now — with your eyes closed —do you truly understand it?

Because sight shows you the world.

But touch teaches you the world.

And in that moment, you learn something profound:

You can navigate without seeing.

You can move without clarity.

You can learn in the dark.

Your other senses rise to meet the moment.

Your memory awakens.

Your brain maps the space around you.

This is spatial memory.

This is neuroplasticity.

This is trust.

Sometimes you don't need more light.

You need to close your eyes and let the rest of you learn.

And just like your senses guide you in the dark, life has a way of guiding you too — especially on the days that teach you something you didn't expect.

The Day That Teaches You:

Some days you wake up and ask yourself, "How's it going?"

Not in a dramatic way — just checking in with the day, the moment, the direction.

And the truth is, we can only accomplish so much in a single day.

Some days, the victory is simply getting through it.

Other days, the victory is getting through it and realizing something deeper:

Earlier in the week, you made the right call —
even if someone else's ego made it messy at the time.

You learn that not everyone thinks about what's best for the whole.

Some people only think about what's best for themselves.

But you can't let that hold you back.

Because most of the time, the universe has a way of sorting things out.

It reveals the truth in its own timing.

And when what you were striving for finally shows up, the excitement reminds you of why you kept going.

The day teaches you — if you're willing to listen.

Which leads me to a day, actually a few weeks to a month or so, that sparked my discipline through pain.

But not every lesson comes from effort or discipline. Some lessons come from the heart — the kind that stop you in your tracks and force you to feel.

Sometimes Love Stops You

Sometimes love has a way of stopping you in your tracks.

Not because it's wrong, and not because it's right — but because love is its own kind of force. It helps sometimes. It hurts sometimes. And whenever you're trying to change yourself, love can feel like it's either pushing you forward or pulling you under.

There was a person who tried to grow, to improve, to become someone better. But love kept showing up — some days lifting them, some days slowing them, some days confusing them so much they didn't know whether love had their back or not.

They learned something:

Love doesn't always make you feel better.

Love doesn't always hurt.

But to experience love at all is still better than never feeling it.

Some days, love makes you feel everything.

Some days, your goals make you feel nothing.

Both are part of the process.

And just like you sometimes need a break from working out, sometimes you need a break from love too — not to quit, but to breathe, reset, and keep moving forward when you're ready.

And when emotions cloud your vision, you learn another truth: sometimes the only way forward is to move carefully, one step at a time, even when you can't see the whole path.

Running in the Dark

Learning in the dark can best be described as going for a run at night.

When I first started running after sunset, I thought I always needed a headlamp to see my way. In the deep woods, that might be true. But when running through a neighborhood, there is often enough light from the moon, porch lights, or streetlights to see just enough.

What I learned is that my eyes adjust.

I may not see as far ahead, but I can still move forward. The difference is that I slow down. I pay closer attention to the ground beneath my feet. I notice cracks in the sidewalk, changes in terrain, shadows, and landmarks that I might ignore during the day.

Learning in the dark works the same way.

When we don't have all the answers, our instinct is often to stop moving. But growth doesn't require perfect visibility. It requires awareness. Sometimes the best thing we can do is slow down, pay attention, and take the next step.

The darkness forces us to examine our surroundings more carefully. It helps us notice where we need to improve, where to focus our efforts, and what truly matters.

We may not be able to see the entire path ahead, but we can almost always see enough to take the next step.

This isn't just a metaphor — your brain is doing something remarkable when you move through uncertainty.

The Science of Learning in the Dark

When you're learning in the dark — emotionally, mentally, or literally — your brain enters a state neuroscientists call prediction error. That's the gap between what you expected and what actually happened. It feels uncomfortable, but biologically, it's one of the strongest triggers for neuroplasticity. When something doesn't match the pattern, the brain pays closer attention.

Uncertainty increases plasticity. Confusion isn't a sign of failure — it's a sign that your brain is updating. This is why emotional fog, like in Sometimes Love Stops You, slows you down. Your brain is shifting out of autopilot and into awareness.

When visibility drops, the brain releases norepinephrine, a chemical that heightens focus and sharpens your senses. This is the same thing that happens when you run at night. You naturally slow down, pay attention to the ground, and notice details you'd ignore during the day. Your brain is doing that on purpose — it's protecting you by increasing awareness.

Neuroscientist Andrew Huberman explains that uncertainty actually opens the plasticity window. When you don't know what comes next, your brain becomes more flexible, more adaptable, and more willing to update old pathways. That's why "The Day That Teaches You" hits so hard — unexpected lessons stick because the brain is wide open during uncertainty.

The brain doesn't need the whole path to move forward. It only needs the next visible step. This is called a proximal cue — the next thing you can see, sense, or understand. When you're running in the dark, you don't need to see the entire road. You need enough light to take the next step safely.

Learning works the same way.

Identity works the same way.

Growth works the same way.

You don't become the future you by seeing the whole map.

You become the future you by taking the next step in the dark.

And you can see this same pattern in everyday life, especially when you step into something unfamiliar.

Real-World Example: Starting a New Job

Starting a new job can be difficult, even when you're a seasoned veteran in your field.

Every workplace has its own culture, workflow, and group dynamics. You have to figure out where you fit in. You have to learn the people, learn the processes, and learn who to trust. You learn who can help you grow, and you learn how you can help others grow in return.

In the beginning, it can feel overwhelming.

There are new names, new expectations, new routines, and new relationships. It can feel like there is too much to learn all at once.

But this is perfectly normal.

The key is to slow down and focus on growth one day at a time. With repetition, the unfamiliar becomes familiar.

Each day you learn a little more about the job, the people, and the environment around you.

Starting a new job is a lot like learning in the dark.

When you first arrive, you don't know what the work environment will be like. You don't know how people will treat you. You don't know how well the team works together. You don't know what challenges you'll face.

What you do know is that you have the skills and experience that brought you there.

So focus on what you can control. Do your job well. Help the people you're there to serve. Pay attention. Learn. Adapt.

Over time, the darkness fades.

You begin to understand the workflow. You learn your coworkers' strengths. You discover where you fit into the team. What once felt confusing starts to make sense.

That's when you truly begin to learn the job.

Once you understand how learning in the dark works, you can finally apply it to your own growth.

Application To Your Life

Whether you're learning in the dark or learning in the light, the process is the same. The only difference is how clearly you can see the path ahead.

When you start something new, take everything you've learned from previous experiences and bring it with you. Be open to learning new ways of doing things, but also be willing to share what you've learned along the way.

Sometimes a new person brings fresh ideas, new perspectives, and better solutions. By simply showing up with a willingness to learn and contribute, you can help make a workplace more positive, more efficient, and more valuable.

The key is to stay curious.

Use your eyes. Use your ears. Use all of your senses.

Pay attention.

Focus on doing your best each day, and trust that the rest will take care of itself.

You don't need to see the entire path.

You only need enough light to take the next step.

Now it's your turn to explore how these ideas show up in your life.

Reflection Questions:

1. At the end of the day, do you reflect on whether you accomplished what you intended?

When you didn't accomplish everything, what was the root cause? And what became your plan for the next day?

2. Have you ever felt like you were in the dark about how to improve yourself?

When you realized you were unclear, did you stop and reflect — or did you avoid it?

3. Think of a time you doubted yourself but still went through the motions.

Did you come out on top, or did you fail?

If you failed, what did you do the next time differently?

Did you learn from it, or did you give up?

4. When you finally saw your goals clearly, how did the world react to the change in you?

Did people support it, resist it, or watch?

5. When you're navigating in the dark, what do your other senses tell you about yourself?

What do they reveal about your surroundings?

Does any of it scare you — and if so, why?

When you learn to move in the dark, something inside you shifts. You stop fearing what you can't see and start uncovering what's been hidden within you all along. And that's where the next chapter begins.

7

Clark Kent and the Box We Keep Ourselves In

The Treasure in the Sand

Alone in the desert, buried beneath the sands of time, lay a treasure no one had seen for years. Wind after wind had blown across it, covering it deeper and deeper until it disappeared completely — hidden, forgotten, unseen. Sometimes we feel like that treasure.

Covered.

Buried.

Hidden under layers of life, fear, doubt, or the versions of ourselves we created to survive. And sometimes we stay hidden on purpose.

Because being unseen feels safer than being misunderstood, but all it takes is a single gust of wind — one small shift, one small step, one small moment — to begin uncovering what's been buried. The wind keeps blowing.

The sand keeps moving.

And slowly, grain by grain, the treasure begins to emerge.

That's how we emerge, too.

One step at a time.

One choice at a time.

One layer at a time. Until finally, the last grain of sand falls away.

The hourglass flips.

And we rise — changed, uncovered, and ready to begin again… This time, out in the open.

As the treasure begins to emerge, another truth rises with it — the realization that sometimes the thing buried isn't our potential, but our identity. And that brings us to another story.

Clark Kent & The Box We Keep Ourselves In

Think about Clark Kent in *Smallville*. He had every ability anyone could ever dream of — strength, speed, power, purpose. But with all those possibilities came lessons. Lessons of restraint. Lessons of bravery. Lessons about hiding who he truly was because he feared what would happen if the world saw the real him.

And honestly?

Most of us do the same thing.

We hide behind disguises.

Not capes.

Not glasses.

But by suppressing who we really are.

We shrink ourselves because we're afraid people will think we're too much, too intense, too different. We stay inside the box we built for ourselves because it feels safe.

But here's the truth:

At some point, you have to step outside that box. You have to get out of your safe circle and find the people who are like you — the ones who lift you, challenge you, stretch you, and grow with you. If you're a weightlifter, a runner, a writer, or a musician, surround yourself with people who live in that world. People who are better than you in some ways and learning from you in others.

Because growth isn't just about improving yourself.

It's about improving the lives of the people around you.

Clark Kent didn't become Superman alone.

He became Superman because of the people who shaped him — and the people he shaped in return.

And that's the real lesson:

You grow when you stop hiding.

You grow when you find your people.

You grow when you let yourself be who you were always meant to be.

Because hiding isn't just something superheroes do in fiction — it's something real people do every day, often without realizing it. And eventually, there comes a moment when we're ready to step out.

Stepping Out of the Box

Somewhere in the world, there's a man or woman in their thirties or forties who has finally stepped out of the box they once lived in. When we're young, we don't realize we're even in a box. We don't see the walls we built around ourselves — walls made of fear, judgment, insecurity, and the belief that the world won't accept who we really are.

Society doesn't always make it easy to be authentic.

So we shrink.

We hide.

We become a quieter version of ourselves, hoping it keeps us safe.

But with age comes wisdom.

And with wisdom comes the ability to overlook the noise — the opinions, the comments, the expectations. One day, something shifts. You stop caring about who approves and who doesn't. You stop apologizing for existing. You stop dimming your own light.

That's the moment you step outside the box.

Maybe that's you right now.

Maybe you're in the season where your wisdom has finally caught up with your courage. Maybe you're ready to show the world who you truly are — not the version you hid, not the version you edited, but the version you were always meant to become.

And here's the truth:

It's not too late.

It's never too late.

Neuroplasticity doesn't care about age.

Your brain can still change.

Your identity can still evolve.

Your pathways can still be rewired.

All it takes is intention — the willingness to take the first step outside the box and let the real you breathe.

Don't give up on yourself.

You're not behind.

You're just stepping into the world as the person you were always meant to be.

But stepping out doesn't mean we're immune to slipping back into old patterns. Sometimes a new identity wraps around us before we even notice — which leads to the next lesson.

The Black Suit

Sometimes our identity gets covered by something we didn't choose. Think about Spider-Man in the black suit — the symbiote wrapped around him without permission, changing the way he moved, acted, and reacted. Some of the changes felt good.

They made him bold.

They made him unfiltered.

They made him act without hesitation — without fear, without second-guessing, without the weight of other people's opinions. But the problem wasn't the power.
It was the lack of reflection. The black suit amplified everything inside him — the emotion, the impulse, the anger — without giving him space to think. It drowned out the part of him that paused, considered, and chose with intention. And that's what happens to us when we chase a new identity so hard that we stop checking in with ourselves. We stop noticing when we're slipping.

We stop noticing when we're acting from the amygdala instead of the prefrontal cortex — all emotion, no reason. But when the bell rang — when the tone cut through the noise — Spider-Man fought his way out of the symbiote's grip. And when the black suit finally peeled away, he didn't go back to who he was before.

He emerged more himself — but with the ability to reflect, to hold back when needed, to choose instead of react. That's the real lesson: Don't let the version of you that feels powerful take over so completely that you lose the version of you that is wise. Growth isn't about becoming unstoppable.

It's about becoming intentional.

Before anything in your life changes, there's always a moment where something inside you shifts — not enough to be visible yet, but enough to be real. A quiet spark. A small pull. A thought that keeps tapping you on the shoulder, asking to be noticed. That's where every version of you begins.

The seed is the thought.

The spark is the action.

Nutrition is the repetition.

And the harvest is the person you eventually become.

And once you peel away what doesn't belong to you, growth doesn't explode all at once. It arrives gently, rhythmically, like something you learn to trust over time.

The Waves

The Waves

Some days aren't meant to rush.

Some days are meant to ride in like the wind on a quiet beach — slow, steady, unforced.

You sit there watching the waves roll out and come back in, until your breathing matches their rhythm. And as you watch, you realize something simple: progress works the same way. You don't force the ocean.

You don't demand the waves hurry.

You just let them come and go, trusting that each one shapes the shore a little more. When you slow down and trust the process — when you take each action for what it is, without trying to make it everything — those small actions add up.

Just like the waves:
What you put out comes back to you as progress.

These stories aren't just metaphors — they mirror what's happening inside the brain when we hide, emerge, and grow.

The Science of Why We Hide — and How the Brain Helps Us Emerge

Before we ever step outside the box, before we brush off the sand, before we become the next version of ourselves, something deeper is happening inside the brain.

Most people think hiding is a personality flaw.

It isn't.

It's biology.

1. The Brain Builds Boxes for Protection

From childhood through adulthood, the brain forms neural pathways based on:

What kept us safe

What helped us belong

What prevented rejection

What reduced conflict

The amygdala — the brain's threat detector — learns quickly and remembers deeply. If being quiet kept you safe, it remembers. If shrinking yourself kept the peace, it remembers. If hiding your real personality prevents judgment, it remembers.

The brain builds "boxes" out of repeated survival strategies. Not because you're weak — but because your nervous system was trying to protect you.

2. Identity Is a Neural Pattern, Not a Fixed Trait

Neuroscientists like Dr. Lisa Feldman Barrett describe identity as a **prediction loop** — your brain constantly guessing who you need to be in each situation based on past experiences.

That means:

"The quiet version of you" is a neural pattern.

"The hidden version of you" is a neural pattern.

"The bold version of you" is a neural pattern.

"The real you" is a neural pattern.

None of these is permanent.

They're pathways — and pathways can be rewired.

3. Neuroplasticity Doesn't Care About Age

For decades, scientists believed the brain stopped changing after childhood.

Now we know the opposite is true.

Research from Harvard, MIT, and Stanford shows:

New neural pathways can form at any age.

Old pathways can weaken through disuse.

Identity can evolve through repetition.

Courage can be trained.

authenticity can be practiced

You're not stuck with the version of yourself you built at 12, 18, or 25.

Your brain is always updating — if you give it new input.

4. Why We Need People to Grow

Social neuroscience shows that the brain is wired for **co-regulation** — meaning we grow faster when we're around people who model the behaviors we want.

Mirror neurons fire when:

You watch someone lift

You watch someone run.

You watch someone write.

You watch someone lead.

You watch someone live boldly.

Your brain literally rehearses the behavior before you ever try it.

That's why Clark Kent needed people.

That's why we all do.

Growth accelerates when you surround yourself with people who live at the level you're trying to reach.

5. The Moment of Emergence

Every transformation begins with a neurological shift — a tiny spark in the prefrontal cortex that says:

"Maybe I can be more than this."

It's not dramatic.

It's not loud.

It's not cinematic.

It's a whisper.

But that whisper is the beginning of a new neural pathway — the first grain of sand moving off the treasure, the first crack in the box, the first tug on the black suit that doesn't belong to you.

And with repetition, that whisper becomes a voice.

Then a belief.

Then an identity.

6. The Science of Becoming

Growth follows a predictable pattern:

Thought → Action → Repetition → Identity

The *thought* sparks the pathway.

The *action* strengthens it.

The *repetition* wires it.

The *identity* emerges from it.

This is neuroplasticity.

This is rewiring.

This is stepping out of the box — not through force, but through biology.

You're not becoming someone new.

You're uncovering who you were always capable of being.

Once you understand how people, environment, and experience shape your identity, you can finally apply these truths to your own becoming.

Real-World Example: Stepping Outside The Box

When we find ourselves inside a box we've lived in our entire lives, it can be difficult to imagine becoming something different, something greater, or something more.

One of the best ways to grow is to seek out people who are already where you want to be.

If you want to become a better runner, spend time with runners. If you want to become a better leader, learn from leaders. If you want to become a better writer, find people who write. Growth leaves clues, and those who have already walked the path often have lessons to share.

As we grow, we climb another step. In many ways, each step requires us to leave another box behind. The beliefs, habits, and limitations that once defined us may no longer be enough to take us where we want to go.

The process is actually simple, even if it isn't easy.

Seek growth through people, education, real-world experience, and challenges that push you beyond your comfort zone. Learn from those who have achieved what you're working toward. Ask questions. Pay attention. Stay curious.

Because the truth is, it's difficult to get outside the box completely on your own.

Sometimes the fastest path to growth is learning from someone who has already found the door.

Application To Your Life

Sometimes it feels like everyone around you is operating at the same level. You may not have a mentor nearby. You may not know anyone who has achieved the goals you're working toward.

That's okay.

Today, growth is more accessible than ever.

There are books.

There are podcasts.

There are online communities.

There are courses, mentors, and teachers willing to share what they've learned.

Sometimes growth requires reaching beyond your immediate environment. Sometimes it requires stepping outside your comfort zone and looking for wisdom in places you've never considered before.

And sometimes, after years of learning and growing, you realize something surprising:

You've become the person you were once searching for.

When that happens, it's your turn to help someone else step outside their box.

Because growth isn't just about becoming more yourself.

It's about helping others discover who they can become, too.

Reflection Questions:

1. What is the new version of yourself you've kept hidden from the world?

Why have you hidden that version, or stopped trying to become the person you see in your mind?

2. When are you going to brush off the sand, step outside the box you've kept yourself in, and expand into the next version of you?

3. Who are the people throughout your life who shaped you into who you are now?

And who are you going to seek out for help in becoming better?

4. Do the people you surround yourself with build you up, or keep you inside the same box you've been living in?

5. When you slow down and reflect, what new habits are you planning to ride back in with when you return to shore?

Stepping out of the box is only the beginning. Once you emerge, you're faced with everything you left unfinished — the habits, the goals, the versions of yourself you never completed. And that's where the next chapter begins.

8

Despicable Me and the Army of Unfinished Selves

Think about *Despicable Me*: Supervillain Gru and his minions. Now look at it through the lens of growth.

What do you see?

I see a man who has created an entire army of unfinished little best versions of himself. Each yellow minion is an unfinished goal. A project he started but never completed. A version of himself he never fully became.

If he could pull every minion back in—every half-finished attempt, every abandoned idea—and integrate them into one whole Despicable Me, he wouldn't be so despicable. He'd be complete. He'd be one.

But instead, he has hundreds of tiny, chaotic, half-baked versions of himself running around. It's funny on screen, but in real life? It's exhausting. It's unrealistic.

And it's painfully honest.

Because really, how many times has he failed and given up on himself?

Better question:

How many little yellow minions have *you* created?

How many unfinished versions of you are out there—half-started habits, abandoned goals, intentions you never finished?

And what are you going to do to pull them together into your best you?

And those unfinished versions of ourselves don't just show up in our goals — they show up in our identity too.

The Person Who Wasn't a Person

How many times have you heard someone say:

"I'm not a morning person."

"I'm not an afternoon person."

"I'm not a night person."

Eventually, you realize what they're really saying:

"I'm not ready to confront the version of myself I could be."

These people aren't despicable to be around —they're despicable toward themselves, the same way Gru was despicable toward his own life long before he ever became a villain.

They're not avoiding the morning.

They're avoiding the version of themselves who could own the morning.

They're not avoiding the afternoon.

They're avoiding the version of themselves who would have to take action.

They're not avoiding the evening.

They're avoiding the version of themselves who would have to reflect on what they didn't do.

It's not about the time of day.

It's about the unfinished versions of themselves they're dodging.

The "I don't run" version.

The "I don't eat vegetables" version.

The "I don't like discipline" version.

The "I'm not ready" version.

Every excuse becomes a minion—a tiny unfinished self running around your life, pulling levers, pushing buttons, and keeping you from becoming who you're meant to be.

And just like Gru, you can't let your minions run wild.

You confront them.

You gather them.

You take all your unfinished selves —the morning person, the afternoon person, the evening person —
and you combine them into the you that you want to be.

It starts with intention.

It continues with finishing what you started.

And it ends with choosing a different outlook.

You're not a morning person — but you can be.

You're not an afternoon person — but you can be.

You're not an evening person — but you can be.

You can be any version of yourself if you want it badly enough.

And when we avoid the versions of ourselves we could become, we start avoiding the people who might expose that truth, which leads to another pattern.

Rumors

When you enter a new group, a new job, or a new season of life, there are always rumors.

Sometimes they're true.

Sometimes they're not.

Most of the time, they're built on fear, not facts. Instead of meeting someone for themselves, people let a rumor tell them who that person is.

They predict the interaction before it ever happens.

They decide who someone is before they ever shake their hand. But here's the truth no one wants to admit:

People avoid direct, honest people because honesty exposes the unfinished version of themselves they don't want to confront. They don't want to talk to the person who might tell them the truth.

They don't want to face the part of themselves that needs work.

They want to stay the same little minion — the same unfinished self — because changing takes effort.

Changing takes action.

Changing takes confronting the version of yourself you've been avoiding. And the rumor?

The rumor is just a shield to protect the minion from ever having to grow.

Because the moment you stop hiding from yourself, you also stop hiding from the work — and that's where ownership begins.

Ownership: The Puzzle You Build Piece by Piece

Taking ownership of your life is a lot like putting together a puzzle.

Not the easy kind — the kind where the pieces are scattered everywhere, some upside down, some missing, some hiding under the couch.

Just like Gru's minions, the pieces of your life don't line up on their own.

They run in different directions.

They pull your attention everywhere.

They represent the unfinished versions of you — the habits you started, the goals you abandoned, the identities you tried on and never fully became.

Ownership begins when you stop ignoring the mess and start gathering the pieces.

You pick up the habits that fit.

You set aside the ones that don't.

You study the edges of your life — the patterns, the colors, the familiar shapes — and you begin to recognize what belongs to you and what never did.

Some pieces click together easily.

Others take time.

Some you have to search for.

Some you have to create because they were never in the box to begin with.

But slowly, piece by piece, the picture becomes clearer.

Not perfect.

Not finished.

But yours.

That's ownership.

Not the moment the puzzle is complete —
But the decision was to keep putting the pieces together.

And you can see this same pattern in real life, especially when you step into something that scares you.

Real-World Example: The Fear of Public Speaking

I think back to when I was a brand-new dietitian and was asked to go to the mall to talk about nutrition. It was my first time being interviewed on camera.

At the time, I was nervous but also excited. I agreed to interview because I knew the information and wanted to help people. After the interview, I watched myself on television.

That's when I noticed something.

My eyes were drifting everywhere.

Instead of focusing on the reporter, I was watching the people around me. I was distracted by everything happening around me. Looking back, I think I was brave enough to do the interview, but I didn't yet have enough experience to present myself the way I wanted to be perceived.

So I asked the reporter for advice.

They gave me a few simple tips about maintaining eye contact and staying focused during interviews. The next time I was interviewed, I practiced those skills. Then I practiced them again. And again.

Over time, I became more comfortable with public speaking and media interviews.

I also learned something important.

Many of the mistakes we think are huge are barely noticeable to anyone else.

When you're the expert speaking, you notice every pause, every stumble, and every moment where you think you could have said something better. Most people don't notice those things at all. They're focused on the message, not the tiny imperfections.

Fear often comes from imagining problems that nobody else can see.

When it comes to public speaking, preparation is your friend. Speak about topics you know well. Understand the purpose of the interview or presentation. Ask questions beforehand. Make sure you're comfortable with the topic and expectations.

And remember, it's okay to say no to opportunities you're not prepared for.

But it's also okay to say yes when you're ready to grow.

The more you understand what you're walking into, the less there is to fear.

Once you understand how unfinished versions of yourself show up in your actions, you can finally apply this to your own growth.

Application To Your Life

Most people have no idea what's happening inside your head.

They don't know what you're worried about.

They don't know what you're afraid of.

They don't know about every mistake you're convinced you've made.

What they see is someone showing up and trying.

Whether you're giving a presentation, interviewing for a job, asking someone out, starting a business, or pursuing a goal, the same principle applies:

Focus on doing your best.

Act with intention.

Prepare when you can.

Learn from your mistakes.

Then let go of what other people might think.

Growth doesn't come from waiting until you're fearless.

Growth comes from taking action while you're still afraid.

The more often you do that, the smaller the fear becomes.

Now it's your turn to gather your minions, confront your unfinished selves, and step into the version of you that's waiting.

Reflection Questions:

1. How many little minions do you have running around — if any?

2. Have you thought about gathering your minions (your abandoned goals) and finishing them one at a time?

3. When you finish all your abandoned goals, what does that version of you look like?

4. Have you ever been a person who "wasn't a person"? Someone who made excuses because becoming the version of yourself you wanted felt like too much work?

5. When you hear a rumor about someone, do you take it at face value — or do you introduce yourself and find out the truth for yourself?

Once you gather your unfinished selves and take ownership of who you're becoming, you face the next challenge: aligning the outside with the inside. That's where the real transformation begins.

9

Captain America and the Mirror We Avoid

Think about Captain America.

Not the shield.

Not the suit.

Think about Steve Rogers before the serum.

On the outside, he looked weak.

On the inside, he was anything but.

How many times have you looked in the mirror and felt that same mismatch?

The outside version of you not lining up with the inside version, you know, is there?

Steve lived that tension every day.

And so do we.

The bad news?

We don't get a super-soldier serum.

We don't get a shortcut.

And honestly… if we did, would we become Captain America?

Or would we become Red Skull?

Because the serum didn't create character — it amplified it.

It revealed who they already were.

That's why shortcuts can't do the work for you.

That's why no pill can build your character.

That's why real change takes discipline, courage, and honesty with yourself.

Becoming who you're meant to be isn't about transforming overnight.

It's about aligning the outside with the inside — one choice, one action, one day at a time.

And that's where the real problem begins — not with who we are, but with the shortcuts we're tempted to take to become someone else.

The Modern Super Soldier Serum

Captain America stepped into a machine and walked out transformed — stronger, faster, leaner, more powerful. The serum didn't just change his body; it amplified who he already was. In the movie, it looks clean, instant, almost magical.

And that's the problem.

Because today, we're selling our own versions of that chamber.

Not glowing vials.

Not sci-fi machines.

But medications, treatments, and interventions promise to reshape us quickly, quietly, and efficiently.

I don't say this from judgment.

I say it from watching people I care about go through these choices — some with great success, some with consequences they never saw coming. I say it from understanding how tempting transformation looks when you're hurting or desperate to change.

But the truth is this:

Every path has a cost, even if the commercial doesn't show it.

Treatments can alter appetite, motivation, or physiology.

Medications can alter how the body communicates with itself.

Interventions can change the mechanics of how we function.

But none of them can change who we are.

The deeper issue isn't the tools themselves.

It's the story wrapped around them.

We're told that transformation should be fast.

That the hard way is outdated.

That the slow path is unnecessary.

That the work of becoming can be bypassed with the right prescription.

But Captain America wasn't great because of the serum.
He was great because of the character he built before he ever stepped into that chamber.

That's the part we forget.

And that's the part no medication, no treatment, no miracle solution can replicate.

So the question becomes:

Do we want to change our bodies at any cost — or do we want to become the kind of person who can sustain the change?

Everyone has to answer that for themselves.

But for me, the line is clear:

I don't want to chemically or surgically alter the way my body works just to fit a world that could accept me as I am — or as I could become through my own effort.

Shortcuts can change your appearance.

Only work can change your identity.

And identity is the only transformation that lasts.

But beyond the stories and metaphors, there's a deeper truth — one rooted in biology, not fantasy.

The Science Of The Modern Superhero Serum

Take a look at the people in your life — the ones you haven't seen in a while, the ones who show up months later looking like a different version of themselves. Not because they stepped into a chamber, not because they took a miracle serum, but because they put in the work.

They're the real-world before-and-after stories.

The ones who lost weight, built muscle, rebuilt confidence, and reshaped their identity through discipline.

When you see them again, it almost feels like they stepped out of the same machine Steve Rogers did — but they didn't get there overnight.

We're all born with certain genetics, certain tendencies, certain environments that shape us.

But as we grow, our choices shape us even more:

What we feed our bodies.
How we move.
The habits we build.
The environments we stay in or escape.
The behaviors we repeat.

All of it becomes the architecture of who we are.

Neuroscientist Joseph LeDoux puts it:

"We are not born with a fixed self. We become who we are through the wiring of experience."

That wiring is built through repetition — not shortcuts.

And when we finally decide to change, we stand at a crossroads:

Not an easy path versus a hard path.

But two hard paths:

The path supported by treatments.

The path supported by discipline alone.

Both require courage.

Both require sacrifice.

Both require honesty.

Both require work.

Do I take a medication or treatment that promises to help, knowing it may come with side effects, unknowns, and the reality that even with assistance, discipline is still required?

Or do I take the long road — the one with setbacks, relapses, and obstacles — and learn how to navigate each one?

Because the hard road is like patching a bucket full of holes.

You fix one leak, then another, then another.

Slowly, the bucket holds more water.

Slowly, the work compounds.

Slowly, the identity changes.

And eventually, the person who steps out on the other side looks like Steve Rogers emerging from the chamber — not because of a serum, but because of consistency, resilience, and the slow, steady rewiring of their own brain.

This isn't just philosophy — it's biology.

Harvard Medical School notes:

"Habits are formed when repeated behaviors create lasting changes in neural pathways."

The American Psychological Association adds:

"Long-term behavior change depends on identity change — not willpower alone."

And Harvard Health reminds us:

"Treatments can influence appetite, motivation, and physiology — but they do not replace the behavioral and psychological work required for lasting change."

That's powerful.

But it's not identity.

It's not a habit.

It's not the wiring that keeps you steady when life hits hard.

No pill builds the neural pathways that keep you on target.

No treatment builds the habits that hold you steady.

No intervention builds the identity that sustains the transformation.

Only work does that.

Only repetition does that.

Only choosing your hard path — again and again — does that.

And that's something worth sitting with.

Worth digesting.

Worth understanding before you choose your path.

And you can see this same pattern in the real world, especially when you look at how people actually transform over time.

Real-World Example: The Work Behind The Scenes

Building strength isn't something that happens from a few workouts or even a few months in the gym. It requires the right amount of protein, training, recovery, and, most importantly, time.

When people see a before-and-after picture, they only see two moments.

They don't see the thousands of repetitions between those moments.

They don't see the early mornings.

They don't see the workouts during lunch breaks.

They don't see the evening training sessions after a long day.

They don't see the runs in the rain.

They don't see the runs in the dark.

They don't see the days when motivation disappeared, but discipline showed up anyway.

They don't see the meals prepared ahead of time, the extra protein, the recovery, the patience, or the consistency.

They see the first and second pictures.

What they don't see is that no secret potion created the transformation.

No superhero serum did the work.

The transformation happened because someone kept showing up.

One workout.

One meal.

One choice.

One day at a time.

Eventually, time caught up with the effort.

A year passed.

Then another.

And the person looking back from the mirror wasn't the same person who started.

Not because they found a shortcut.

Because they built themselves through repetition.

Once you understand what real transformation requires, you can finally apply it to your own journey.

Application to Your Life

In life, there are always shortcuts being advertised.

Shortcuts to lose weight.

Shortcuts to get rich.

Shortcuts to build confidence.

Shortcuts to success.

Some shortcuts may provide temporary results, but they rarely teach the lessons that create lasting change.

Discipline cannot be borrowed.

Confidence cannot be purchased.

Resilience cannot be downloaded.

Those qualities are earned through repeated action over time.

Real work teaches patience.

Real effort teaches discipline.

Real consistency teaches resilience.

The process itself becomes the reward because every step forward strengthens the person who takes it.

The truth is simple:

There is no superhero serum.

There is only the person you become through the choices you make every day.

And that person is far more powerful than any shortcut could ever be.

Now it's your turn to explore what transformation means for you — without shortcuts, without serums, and without rushing the process.

Reflection Questions:

1. Have you looked in the mirror and seen the version of yourself you want to be?

If not, imagine who you want to become, the steps it takes, and compare that to who you are now and who you were before.

2. Have you ever thought about taking a shortcut to hit your goals?

If you took it, what was the outcome — and how did it make you feel?

3. When you chose not to take the shortcut and instead took the real steps, did you get there?

How did it feel looking back on the experience?

4. When you decided what needed to change, how many holes did you find in your bucket?

And how are you going to patch them?

5. What habit are you going to change — and will you be intentional with the actions you take?

Once you understand that real transformation comes from repetition, not shortcuts, the next step is learning how the brain actually builds that change. And that's where the science becomes powerful.

10

Neuroplasticity as Teamwork

Neuroplasticity is a lot like teamwork. When you have a highly cohesive team, communication flows. Signals are clear. Everyone knows their role. That's a highly myelinated pathway — fast, smooth, efficient.
But superiority? Cliques? Side-agendas?

That's the downfall of teams.

A clique inside a team is like dropping a pile of bricks in the middle of a neural pathway. The communication doesn't flow. The signals get blocked. The team keeps defaulting to what's familiar, even if it's not what's best.

Habits work the same way.

Old habits are the cliques — they stick together, they resist change, and they like doing things the way they've always done them. They're the "we've always done it this way" crowd inside your brain.

It takes a good manager to break up the cliques and get the whole team co-elevating again.

And just like that, it takes motivation, discipline, and repetition to start a new habit and break an old one.

Every time you repeat the new behavior, you're strengthening the new team.

You're improving communication.

You're laying down myelin.

You're building cohesion.

And eventually, the new team becomes the one that runs the show.

And once you understand how habits behave like teams, it becomes even clearer when you look at how the brain learns physical skills.

The Baseball Brain — Why Repetition Works

Think of a young baseball player learning how to catch and throw a ball.

There are so many systems at play, it's almost unbelievable.

Touch:

Feeling the ball, the seams, the weight, the texture.
Vision:

Tracking distance, angle, arc, velocity, and timing the release.

Body mechanics:

Arm slot, shoulder rotation, finger release, follow-through.

Catching is its own universe:

The feel of the glove, the pocket, the padding, the timing of the squeeze.

Every one of these actions requires the brain to build **neural pathways** — nerve cells created specifically for that purpose.

And the only way those pathways form?

Repetition

You repeat the behavior until the skill exists.

Then you refine the skill until it becomes automatic.

Then you refine the automatic until it becomes elite.

That's how professionals are made — through highly clustered, heavily myelinated nerve fibers that fire faster than you can blink.

Repetition isn't boring.

Repetition is biology.

Repetition is transformation.

Learning a new skill isn't just about your brain. It's your whole body.

Your nerves, your muscles, your lungs, your heart — even your kidneys are in on it.

But more than anything, it's **intention**.

It's heart.

And when I say heart, I mean the effort you bring, the love you put into the reps.

Every new skill begins the same way:

A spark of electricity — an action potential — firing down a nerve.

That spark becomes a throw, a swing, a sprint, a first mile, a first home run, a perfect throw from the outfield to third.

And none of it happens without repetition.

Repetition strengthens the pathway.

Strengthening the pathway means insulating the axon.

Every rep adds another layer of insulation — **myelin** — much like wrapping tape around a wire makes the signal travel faster.

Myelination is like giving your body pre-workout without taking anything at all.

The fuel is effort.

The stimulant is consistency.

Every rep is another wrap.

Every wrap makes the signal quicker.

Every quicker signal makes the movement smoother.

Your fine motor skills sharpen.

Your muscles fire more efficiently.

Your coordination improves.

Your awareness expands.

Your timing gets cleaner.

Your sense of space gets sharper.

The more you do it, the more automatic it becomes.

The more automatic it becomes, the better you get. And the better you get, the closer you are to becoming the new you.

But repetition doesn't just shape skills — it shapes identity. And sometimes that identity grows quietly, waiting for its moment.

The Lonely Fruit

There once was a lonely fruit hanging on a tree.

He started out small, just like all the others, and slowly grew into one of the most delicious-looking fruits on the branch.

One by one, he watched his friends get picked.

One by one, he watched them fall.

One by one, he watched them leave the tree while he remained — the last one hanging, waiting for his moment.

He felt alone up there.

He wondered when his opportunity would come.

He wondered if he had already missed it.

Because if he stayed too long, he knew what would happen:

His growth would stop, his sweetness would fade, and everything he had become would slowly rot away.

So he made a choice.

A small one.

A simple one.

A brave one.

He shifted himself toward the sun.

And the sun responded.

It warmed him, brightened him, deepened his color, and revealed the beauty of the growth he had worked so hard for.

When someone finally came along, they noticed him immediately.

He wasn't picked first — but he was picked last, and sometimes the last ones are the best ones.

The last ones are disciplined.

The last ones are thoughtful.

The last ones know what it feels like to be overlooked — and that makes them strong in ways others never had to be.

It's okay to wait after you've grown.

It's okay to take your time.

But don't wait so long that you lose what you've become.

Know when to step into the sunlight.

Know when to take your chance.

And when the moment is right, let yourself be seen.

And while some growth happens in the sunlight, other lessons come from fear — especially the kind we don't fully understand at first.

The Chicken & The Potato

Once upon a time, people ate chickens as chickens.

And as we slowly begin to change — as we grow into who we truly are and who we're meant to become — something strange happens. We start forgetting who we were and remembering who we are. And that scares us.

Not because we finally made it, but because now we have to keep doing everything it took to get here. Because if we stop, we slip right back to where we started. And that fear makes sense in the world we live in now — a world where things aren't always what they seem. A world where food is twisted, turned, dehydrated, and spit back out into forms it was never meant to be. If the world can do that to a chicken, imagine what it can do to a person who isn't paying attention.

Then the world got busy, and chickens became chips — flattened, fried, flavored, and forgotten.

And somewhere in the middle of all that, the potatoes rolled over, looked at the chicken chips, and said, "bok bok." Because when you change something enough times, even the things around it start forgetting what they were supposed to be.

There once was a chicken who was, well… a chicken.

He was afraid of everything.

Afraid to go outside.

Afraid to lay the egg.

Afraid of being eaten.

Afraid of the world.

Afraid, without even knowing why he was afraid.

Every morning, he woke up the same way:

"Bok bok bok… I'm coming, I'm coming.

I'm starting my day.

I'm scared.

I'm scared.

I'm scared."

Day after day, the same fear.

The same panic.

The same trembling start.

Until one day, the chicken finally learned the truth.

He wasn't scared because he was weak.

He wasn't scared because he was broken.

He wasn't scared because he was "just a chicken."

He was scared because he was about to be picked.

Picked for something he didn't want.

Picked for something he wasn't ready for.

Picked for something that didn't fit who he was.

And when he got picked, he learned the harshest truth of all:

Not everything you're chosen for is good for you.

Not every opportunity is meant to be taken.

Not every path is meant to be walked.

The chicken who got picked… got cooked.

So the lesson is simple:

Be careful what you say yes to.

Be careful what you let choose you.

Be careful what you allow yourself to be "picked" for.

Because, unlike the chicken, you have a choice.

If something doesn't feel right,

If something doesn't align with who you are,

if something scares you because it's wrong —
You can turn away.

You don't have to get picked.

You don't have to get cooked.

You don't have to be afraid of the wrong things anymore.

But why was the chicken scared in the first place?

Why does fear show up before we even understand it?

It turns out the chicken is teaching us something about our own brains.

A chicken doesn't know why it's scared.

It just knows that chickens go missing. One disappears, then another, then another.

Its brain records only one truth:

"When something comes for you, you don't come back."

That fear is wired into its biology.

Because beneath the story of the chicken is a deeper truth about how fear actually works inside the brain.

The Science of Fear

Neuroscientist Joseph LeDoux discovered that the amygdala fires before the thinking brain even knows what's happening.

That means fear hits first, understanding comes later — if it comes at all.

A chicken doesn't get to pause.

It doesn't get to reflect.

It doesn't get to choose.

It just gets plucked.

Chickens don't have a developed prefrontal cortex — the part of the brain responsible for planning, intention, and self-control.

Humans do.

And according to Harvard Medical School, the prefrontal cortex is the only part of the brain capable of calming the amygdala once fear fires.

That's the difference.

We feel fear the same way a chicken does — fast, automatic, protective — but we also have the ability to pause, reflect, and choose.

That pause is the prefrontal cortex stepping in to override instinct.

And here's where it gets deeper:

Some fear doesn't come from your life at all.

It comes from the lives before you.

Research by Rachel Yehuda shows that trauma can be passed

down through generations — encoded in stress hormones, gene expression, and nervous system patterns.
Your body can react to things your mind has never experienced, because someone in your lineage did.

Fear can be inherited.

Fear can be predicted.

Fear can be awakened by sensory cues you don't consciously recognize.

Your environment shapes you.

Your past shapes you.

Your ancestors shape you.

And the only way to reshape fear is through neuroplasticity — the brain's ability to rewire itself through repetition. As Harvard's research on neuroplasticity shows, new neural pathways form when you repeatedly practice new behaviors, new thoughts, and new responses.

That's why preparation matters.

That's why pausing matters.

That's why intention matters.

The chicken was scared because fear was programmed into it.

It didn't know why.

It didn't have a choice.

It didn't have a prefrontal cortex.

It didn't have agency.

But you do.

You're not a chicken.

You're not being plucked out of your environment without warning.

You're not powerless.

If you prepare yourself — mentally, emotionally, intentionally — there is nothing to be afraid of.

Fear fires first.

You choose what happens next.

And once you understand how fear fires and how choice intervenes, you can finally see the rhythm behind real growth.

Cycle of Change

There's a cycle we all move through when we're trying to grow:

Intention → Action → Repetition → Recovery.

When the cycle is in sync, everything feels smooth.
But sometimes one part slips out of rhythm — maybe the

recovery doesn't happen, maybe the repetition gets interrupted, maybe the intention gets cloudy. When that happens, the whole system feels off. And that's not failure. That's a signal. It means something needs to be adjusted, refined, or rebalanced so the cycle can flow again.

Nature works the same way.

Plants need water to grow — but not too much.

A little water nourishes.

Too much water drowns.

Lakes, rivers, and oceans hold massive amounts of water, but when the balance tips, floods happen. Water spills into places it was never meant to go. New pathways form, not because they were intended, but because the system was overwhelmed. Damage happens when the cycle is overloaded.

Growth is no different.

If you push too hard without recovery, you flood yourself.

If you stay too caught up in the moment, you drown your own progress.

If you never pause, you never heal.

So remember: give yourself enough — enough effort, enough intention, enough repetition — but also enough space to breathe. Growth needs balance. Healing is part of the cycle. And just like nature, you grow best when you're watered just right.

And the potato was meant to be hot, hot, hot, not go bok, bok, bok.

This same rhythm shows up in everyday life, especially when you look at how real teams function — and how people grow together.

Real-World Example: Effective Communication

A highly functional team communicates effectively, shows appreciation, refines its processes, and focuses on continuous growth. Team members celebrate wins, own failures, and learn from mistakes rather than hiding from them.

I've been part of many teams throughout my life.

On a team, you usually do one of four things:

You lead.

You follow.

You do both.

Or you sit back and drain the energy from everyone around you.

The strongest teams understand that success isn't about any one individual. It's about people working together toward a common goal.

Growth works the same way.

Just as an effective team communicates, adapts, and improves, we must learn to work with ourselves in the same way. We have strengths, weaknesses, habits, emotions, and experiences that all influence our decisions. The more those parts work together, the more effective we become.

A great team isn't built overnight.

Neither is a great life.

Both are built through communication, trust, accountability, and continuous improvement.

And just like a team, your own growth depends on how well the different parts of you work together.

Application to Your Life

Wherever you find yourself today, you can apply the principles of teamwork to your own growth.

Think of your past self, your current self, and your future self as members of the same team.

Your past self provides lessons.

Your current self takes action.

Your future self receives the rewards of those actions.

When those versions of yourself work together, growth becomes possible.

The choices you make today become gifts to your future self. The lessons you learned yesterday become tools you can use today.

Teamwork is more than working well with other people.

It's learning to work well with yourself.

Every day you are changing.

Every day you are becoming someone new.

And every day presents another opportunity to learn, improve, and grow.

The most effective team you will ever be part of is the one that exists between who you were, who you are, and who you are becoming.

Now it's your turn to explore how teamwork, fear, repetition, and intention shape the person you're becoming.

Reflection Questions:

1. Have you ever been part of a dysfunctional team?

2. Have you ever been part of a highly cohesive team?

3. If you've experienced both, what differences did you notice between them?

4. Have you ever been the last one picked?

How did it feel — and what did you do to change yourself so you'd be picked earlier next time?

5. Once you've completed all the steps to become the next version of yourself, how does that version of you show up?

After all the teamwork, the rewiring, the repetition, and the choices you've made along the way, something becomes clear: growth isn't just happening in your habits — it's happening in your identity. And when all the versions of you finally begin working together, you're ready to step into the final truth this book has been leading you toward.

Conclusion

Finally, the path forward began to shine — the new version of yourself stepping out of its comfort zone, resilience burning like the brightest star in the galaxy.

Throughout this book, you've seen me connect ideas to movies, TV shows, cartoons, teamwork, and even the dance between Eb and Flow. But here's the truth:

It doesn't take a story.

It doesn't take a parable.

It just takes you opening your eyes to how everything connects.

We're all connected in one way or another.

We all walk different paths.

And inside our minds, we all carry different neural pathways —

some built in childhood, some built through repetition, some built through survival, some built through love.

Those pathways were shaped long before we could remember anything.

But our cells remember.

Our nervous system remembers.

Our brain remembers.

And those pathways will always be there — unless something traumatic rewires them.

But that's the beauty of neuroplasticity:

If change is possible, the brain will find a way.

Your brain — and the nerve cells inside it — take into account your environment, your genetics, your effort, your chemistry, and your experiences… all of that just to help you pick up a weight, move it up and down, and get stronger with every rep.

So if you take nothing else from this book, take this:

Repetition is the key that opens the doorway.

The doorway to new habits.

The doorway to discipline.

The doorway to resilience.

The doorway to change.

And once you understand that repetition opens the doorway, you're ready for the deeper truth behind it — the truth about how every version of you works together to create the person you're becoming. That's where the Fig Brain comes in.

Afterword

Growth isn't something that happens in a straight line.

It isn't a single breakthrough or a single moment of clarity.

It's a symbiotic process, just like the fig and the fig wasp — two forces working together to create something neither can do alone.

You don't need the biology lesson to understand the heart of it.

All you need to know is this:

The fig and the fig wasp need each other to survive.

And in the same way, you need every version of yourself to grow.

That's the Fig Brain.

The Three Selves That Make Growth Possible

1. Past Self

Your past self is the root system.

It holds the lessons, the patterns, the pain, the survival strategies.

It's not something to run from — it's something to learn from.

2. Present Self

Your present self is the fig — the container where growth actually happens.

It's the honesty, the awareness, the choices you make right now.

This is where transformation becomes real.

3. Future Self

Your future self is the fig wasp — the spark, the pollinator, the direction.

It's the version of you that pulls you forward and activates change.

The Truth of the Fig Brain

Growth happens when:

Your past self gives you wisdom.
Your present self gives you honesty.
Your future self gives you direction.

Just like the fig and the wasp, each part of you needs the others.

That's why the Fig Brain isn't just a metaphor.

It's a model for transformation.

It's the foundation of co-self elevation —
all versions of you working together to elevate the whole.

Growth is a symbiotic relationship between who you were, who you are, and who you're becoming.

All three must work together for you to evolve.

The Growth Toolkit

Congratulations on finishing. *Let Yourself Grow.*

Throughout this book, you've explored stories, science, reflections, and lessons designed to help you think differently about growth.

Understanding growth is important, but growth happens through action.

The following worksheets are designed to help you apply the concepts from this book to your own life. You do not need to complete them all at once. Start with the worksheet that speaks to you most and use it as a tool to take your next step forward.

Remember: growth does not happen overnight. It happens through small actions repeated consistently over time.

Now it's your turn.

Let yourself grow.

The Pickle Parable Worksheet

The Pickle Parable Worksheet

A cucumber does not become a pickle overnight. It changes because of what surrounds it.

People are no different. The people we spend time with, the content we consume, the habits we practice, and the environments we place ourselves in all influence who we become.

What 'jar' am I sitting in right now?

____

____

What influences am I exposed to every day?

People: ________________________________

Media: _________________________________

Habits: ______________________________

Environment: ______________________________

Is my current jar helping me grow?

■ Yes ■ Somewhat ■ No

Why?

____

Which parts of my environment help me improve?

____

____

What parts of my environment hold me back?

____

____

If I continue in this jar for the next five years, where will I end up?

____

____

What changes can I make to my jar?

People to spend more time with: ______________________________

Habits to strengthen: ______________________________

Distractions to reduce: ______________________________

New influences to add: ______________________________

My Growth Ingredients

■ Discipline ■ Courage ■ Patience ■ Kindness ■ Consistency
■ Curiosity ■ Gratitude ■ Resilience ■ Other: __________

Reflection

What kind of person am I becoming based on what surrounds me today?

____

____

My Commitment

I will intentionally choose the environment that shapes my future.

Signature: ____________________________

Date: __________________________________

Top of The Molehill Worksheet

The Top of the Molehill

Growth rarely happens all at once. At first, every step feels difficult. Progress seems slow. The Meadow of Minions behind you is filled with distractions, excuses, self-doubt, fear, procrastination, and old habits trying to pull you back down. But every small step matters.

What valley am I trying to leave behind?

____

____

____

____

____

What minions are holding me back?

■ Fear ■ Self-Doubt ■ Procrastination ■ Comfort ■ Distraction

■ Perfectionism ■ Lack of Confidence ■ Other: ___________

What does my molehill look like?

____
____
____
____

What small step can I take today?

____
____
____
____

What obstacles might I face on the climb?

____
____
____
____

How will I respond when I encounter those obstacles?

____
____
____
____

How will I know I've reached the top of this molehill?

____
____
____
____

Reflection

What will be different in my life once I leave this meadow behind?

____

____

____

____

My Commitment

Today I choose to take one step higher.

Signature: ____________________

Date: ________________________

The Next Attempt Worksheet

The Next Attempt Worksheet

Elmer Fudd, Wiley Coyote, and Foghorn Leghorn all teach the same lesson: failure is not the end of
the story. Every setback contains information. Growth happens when we learn, adjust, and make
another attempt.

What am I chasing?

____

____

What setbacks have I encountered?

____

____

What have those setbacks taught me?

____

____

What would Wiley Coyote do?

■ Quit ■ Try another plan

What would Elmer Fudd do?

■ Give up ■ Keep hunting

What would Foghorn Leghorn say?

"I say, I say..."

____

____

What's my next attempt?

____

When will I make it? _________________________

What did I learn from my last failure?

____

____

What will I do differently this time?

____

____

My Commitment

I understand that failure is information. I will use what I learn and make another attempt.

Signature: ________________________

Date: ______________________________

The Past Self, Present Self and Future Self Worksheet

Past Self, Present Self, Future Self

The Fig Brain Worksheet

Growth happens across time. Your past has shaped you. Your present choices define you. Your future self is being built one action at a time. Use this worksheet to connect all three.

Past Self

What experiences shaped me into who I am today?

____

____

What lessons should I carry forward?

____

Present Self

Where am I right now?

What challenge am I currently facing?

What strengths can I use?

Future Self

Who am I becoming?

What would my future self thank me for doing today?

The Fig Brain

What pathway am I strengthening?

What pathway am I weakening?

What seed am I planting today?

Reflection

If my Past Self, Present Self, and Future Self sat together under the Fig Brain, what advice would
they give me?

____

____

____

My Commitment

I will learn from my past.

I will act in the present.

I will build my future.

Signature: __________________________

Date: ______________________________

The Build One Pathway Worksheet

Build One Pathway

Every thought, habit, and action travels along a pathway in your brain. The pathways you use repeatedly become stronger. Growth does not happen by changing everything at once. Growth happens by building one pathway at a time.

The Pathway I Want to Build

What is the ONE habit, thought, belief, or behavior I want to strengthen?

____

____

Why Does This Matter?

____

____

My Current Pathway

What do I usually do right now?

____

____

My New Pathway

What will I do instead?

____

____

My Trigger

After I ______________________________

At ___________________________________

When _______________________________

Repetition Strengthens the Path

■1 ■2 ■3 ■4 ■5 ■6 ■7 ■8 ■9 ■10

■11 ■12 ■13 ■14 ■15 ■16 ■17 ■18 ■19 ■20

Obstacles Along the Path

____

____

My Response Plan

____

____

Reflection

How will strengthening this pathway improve my life?

____

____

Future Self Check-In

If I repeat this pathway for the next year, what could change?

____

____

My Commitment

I will focus on one pathway.

I will strengthen it through repetition.

I will trust the process.

Signature: __________________________

Date: _______________________________

Final Note to The Reader

My final words to you are this:

No Matter what it is that you want to accomplish, start small and work at it every day with intention.

Growth rarely happens overnight. It happens through consistent actions repeated over time.

Keep learning.

Keep trying.

Keep growing.

And most importantly, let yourself grow.

About the Author

Daniel Jarvis is a registered dietitian, Air Force veteran, runner, and author who believes that growth is one of the most powerful forces in life.

His passion is helping people move forward, not by telling them what to do, but by encouraging them to become a little better each day through stories, science, reflection, and practical application. He hopes to inspire others to embrace growth in their own lives.

When he's not writing, Daniel is doing his best to live the principles he teaches, enjoys exercising, weightlifting, running, working as a dietitian, making healthy choices, making mistakes, learning from them, and intentionally working to become a better version of himself.

He is fascinated by the brain's ability to adapt and change through neuroplasticity and believes that small, consistent action can lead to a remarkable transformation over time. He hopes that this book encourages you to take the next step forward and reminds you that growth is always possible. Remember, growth is not a destination; it is a lifelong journey.

www.ingramcontent.com/pod-product-compliance
Lightning Source LLC
LaVergne TN
LVHW030725061126
851857LV00019B/2001
* 9 7 9 8 2 3 4 1 8 2 3 6 4 *